Volume equivalents

METRIC	IMPERIAL	METRIC	IMPERIAL
30ml	1fl oz	450ml	15fl oz
60ml	2fl oz	500ml	16fl oz
75ml	2$\frac{1}{2}$fl oz	600ml	1 pint
100ml	3$\frac{1}{2}$fl oz	750ml	1$\frac{1}{4}$ pints
120ml	4fl oz	900ml	1$\frac{1}{2}$ pints
150ml	5fl oz ($\frac{1}{4}$ pint)	1 litre	1$\frac{3}{4}$ pints
175ml	6fl oz	1.2 litres	2 pints
200ml	7fl oz ($\frac{1}{3}$ pint)	1.4 litres	2$\frac{1}{2}$ pints
250ml	8fl oz	1.5 litres	2$\frac{3}{4}$ pints
300ml	10fl oz ($\frac{1}{2}$ pint)	1.7 litres	3 pints
350ml	12fl oz	2 litres	3$\frac{1}{2}$ pints
400ml	14fl oz	3 litres	5$\frac{1}{4}$ pints

Weight equivalents

METRIC	IMPERIAL	METRIC	IMPERIAL
15g	$\frac{1}{2}$oz	150g	5$\frac{1}{2}$oz
20g	$\frac{3}{4}$oz	175g	6oz
25g	scant 1oz	200g	7oz
30g	1oz	225g	8oz
45g	1$\frac{1}{2}$oz	250g	9oz
50g	1$\frac{1}{3}$oz	300g	10oz
60g	2oz	450g	1lb
75g	2$\frac{1}{2}$oz	500g	1lb 2oz
85g	3oz	675g	1$\frac{1}{2}$lb
100g	3$\frac{1}{2}$oz	900g	2lb
115g	4oz	1kg	2$\frac{1}{4}$lb
125g	4$\frac{1}{2}$oz	1.5kg	3lb 3oz
140g	5oz	1.8kg	4lb

everyday easy
Chicken

everyday easy
Chicken

simple suppers • roasts • one-pot • leftovers

DK

LONDON, NEW YORK, MELBOURNE,
MUNICH, AND DELHI

Editor
Andrew Roff

Designer
Kathryn Wilding

Senior Jacket Creative
Nicola Powling

Managing Editor
Dawn Henderson

Managing Art Editor
Christine Keilty

Production Editor
Ben Marcus

Production Controller
Hema Gohil

Creative Technical Support
Sonia Charbonnier

DK INDIA

Head of Publishing
Aparna Sharma

Design Manager
Romi Chakraborty

Designer
Neha Ahuja

DTP Co-ordinator
Balwant Singh

DTP Designer
Tarun Sharma

Material first published in *The Cooking Book* in 2008
This edition first published in Great Britain in 2009
by Dorling Kindersley Ltd
80 Strand, London WC2R 0RL

This edition published in 2009 for Index Books Ltd

A Penguin Company
Copyright © 2008, 2009 Dorling Kindersley
Text copyright © 2008, 2009 Dorling Kindersley

2 4 6 8 10 9 7 5 3 1

A CIP catalogue record for this book
is available from the British Library.

ISBN 978-1-4053-4103-5

Colour reproduction by MDP, Bath
Printed and bound in Singapore by Star Standard

Discover more at
www.dk.com

CONTENTS

We all love chicken. You'll find a classic chicken dish where-ever you happen to be – be it Chicken Tikka Masala in India, Southern Fried Chicken in the southern states of America, or Thai Noodle Stir-fry in Thailand. It's great news then that most of these are easy to make at home when you're shown how. Chicken is great for any occasion too – from a fast family supper to an impressive main when entertaining – so knowing your wishbone from your drumstick can drastically increase your culinary repertoire. Easy to cook, healthy, and readily available, the benefits of being a chicken whiz are manifold.

Other poultry is equally delicious, so we've included some here too. Turkey, goose, poussin, and duck are all readily available and are worth the extra expense. Game meats, such as pheasant and guinea fowl, although more occasional dishes, are thoroughly rewarding to cook and eat.

A range of chicken **Techniques** at the beginning of the book, including jointing, boning, spatchcocking, marinating, poaching, braising, roasting, and carving, will refine your core skills, enabling you to save time in the kitchen. Following this is a range of **Recipe Choosers** that showcase recipes Ready in 30 Minutes, Healthy, Budget, Prepare Ahead, Spicy, or Light so cooks in a hurry can easily find something suitable.

A selection of moreish nibbles and bite-sized finger food in the **Eat With Your Fingers** section gives great ideas for starting a meal when entertaining, creating an informal buffet, or taking on a picnic. Serve Chicken Liver Pâté to guarantee a flying start to an informal dinner party or add Chicken Croustades to a help-yourself-style party tea – sure to be the most popular dish on the table.

Simple Suppers includes recipes that you can easily make in the evening on a hectic weekday, including Chicken in Garlic Sauce, Chicken Jalfrezi, and Devilled Turkey. These recipes require just a few ingredients and take minimal time to prepare. Simple and tasty – these are guaranteed to become family favourites that you can whip up in no time.

If you want to enjoy a delicious meal without having to wash lots of dishes afterwards, choose something from the **One-pot** section. Coq au Vin and Chicken Pot Pie are particular one-pot classics. Put all the ingredients together in a pot, leave to bubble in the oven or on the hob, and wait for the mouth-watering results.

Chicken can impress too and can be the perfect choice to cook for friends. It partners well with a number of flavours, in dishes such as Chicken with Pancetta, and textures, in dishes such as Creamy Tarragon Chicken, to give many luxurious meals, all on offer in the **Supper for Friends** section.

For many people, a Sunday wouldn't be the same without a roast and with the wealth of recipes on offer in the **Roasts** section, why save it for just one day a week? Make any of these classic roast recipes, including Roast Chicken and Chicken in a Pot, or try something a little different – treat the family to French Roast Chicken or Roast Chicken with Lemon and Thyme.

If you plan your meals you can easily make a whole chicken last several days. Make one of the recipes in the **Leftovers** section, such as Calzone or Chicken Pasties, great for using up any remaining poultry or other leftover ingredients in the fridge. A meal made from leftovers can often be as great as the meal that produced them!

Add some vegetables or other side dishes to your meal with the recipes in the **Accompaniments** section, including Ultimate Mashed Potato and Egg Fried Rice, and you have everything you need to make a spectacular chicken dinner.

Give all of these recipes a try and see just how easy it is to enjoy chicken and other poultry every day.

A guide to symbols

The recipes in this book are accompanied by symbols that alert you to important information.

 Tells you how many people the recipe serves, or how much is produced.

 Indicates how much time you will need to prepare and cook a dish. Next to this symbol you will also find out if additional time is required for such things as marinating, standing, or cooling. You will have to read the recipe to find out exactly how much extra time is needed.

 Points out nutritional benefits, such as low fat or low GI.

 This is especially important, as it alerts you to what has to be done before you can begin to cook the recipe. For example, you may need to soak some beans overnight.

 This denotes that special equipment is required, such as a deep-fat fryer or skewers. Where possible, alternatives are given.

 This symbol accompanies freezing information.

Roasting Poultry

Use these times as a guide, bearing in mind the size and weight of each bird vary. Be sure to preheat the oven before cooking your bird(s), and always check that the bird is fully cooked before serving.

MEAT		OVEN TEMPERATURE	COOKING TIME
Poussin		190°C (375°F/Gas 5)	12 mins per 450g (1lb) plus 12 mins
Chicken		200°C (400°F/Gas 6)	20 mins per 450g (1lb) plus 20 mins
Duck		180°C (350°F/Gas 4)	20 mins per 450g (1lb) plus 20 mins
Goose		180°C (350°F/Gas 4)	20 mins per 450g (1lb) plus 20 mins
Pheasant		200°C (400°F/Gas 6)	50 mins total cooking
Turkey	3.5–4.5kg (7–9lb)	190°C (375°F/Gas 5)	2½–3 hrs total cooking
	5–6kg (10–12lb)	190°C (375°F/Gas 5)	3½–4 hrs total cooking
	6.5–8.5kg (13–17lb)	190°C (375°F/Gas 5)	4½–5 hrs total cooking

Choosing your chicken

Of all poultry, chicken is the most intensely reared. Age, exercise, and a good diet all add flavour – and it must be said expense – to chickens. Supermarkets and butchers sell many varieties of chicken that reflect all these conditions.

Common labels

Free-range birds cannot be stocked more than 13 per square metre, and should have access to daytime open-air runs for at least half their life.

Traditional Free-range birds must be one of the slow-growing breeds. They cannot be stocked more than 4000 in a house and more than 12 per square metre.

Free-range Total Freedom birds, in addition to the traditional free-range specifications (above), should have unlimited open-air runs.

Organic birds must come from a farm recognized by an organic certification body. They are fed organic grains and soybeans, cannot be treated with drugs, and must have outdoor access.

Common classifications

Stewing chicken are female chickens over 10 months old and weighing over 1.35kg (3lb). They are great for stewing and poaching.

Chicken – depending on whether the bird is organic, free-range, or not, chickens are slaughtered between $5\frac{1}{4}$ to $11\frac{1}{2}$ weeks old. They weigh around 1.5kg (3lb 3oz).

Poussin are young chickens less than 28 days old, weighing 340–450g (12oz–1lb). These are tender birds that are great roasted or spatchcocked on a barbecue.

Put your wrapped bird on a plate with a rim in the bottom of the refrigerator. Don't let any raw juices drip and observe the use-by date.

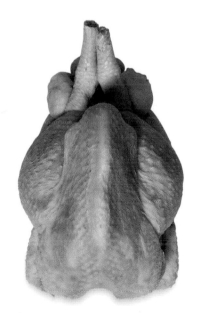

Stewing chicken

Chicken

Poussin

TECHNIQUES

Jointing

Poultry is often left whole for roasting, poaching, and slow-cooking in a pot. For other methods, cut them into 4 or 8 pieces. For 4 pieces, joint to step 6 and for 8 pieces, continue to step 8.

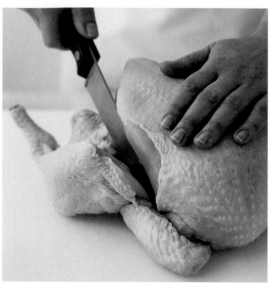

1 Remove the wishbone, then place the bird breast-side up onto a cutting board. Using a sharp knife, cut down and through the thigh joint to separate the leg from the rest of the body.

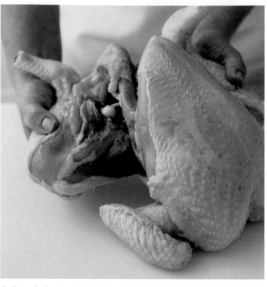

2 Bend the leg back to dislodge the leg joint. When the ball is free from the socket you will hear a pop. Use your knife to cut away any meat still attached to the body. Repeat on the other leg.

3 Fully extend one wing, then use sharp poultry shears to cut off the winglet at the middle joint. Repeat to remove the other winglet.

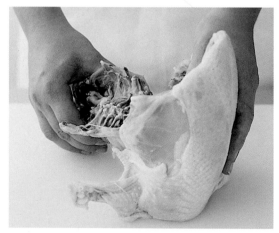

4 Using your hands, firmly grasp the backbone and break it from the crown (the 2 breasts and wings on the bone).

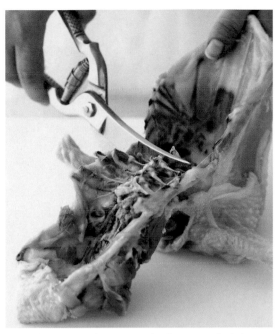

5 Using poultry shears, cut the lower end of the backbone from the remaining body.

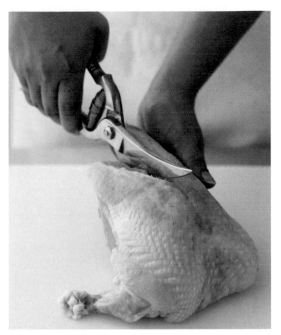

6 Starting at the neck, use poultry shears to cut all the way through the backbone to separate the breasts. The chicken is now cut into 4 pieces.

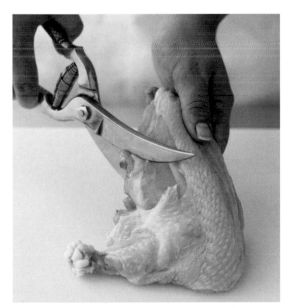

7 Use poultry shears to cut each breast in half diagonally, producing one breast and one wing. Repeat to separate the other breast from the wing.

8 Cut each leg through the knee joint, above the drumstick that connects to the thigh. The chicken is now cut into 8 pieces.

Boning

For quickly braised dishes or recipes that call for poultry to be flattened, the bones must first be removed.

Detach the breast

1 Using poultry shears, work from the thickest wing end of the breast towards the narrowest end and cut away the ribs and the backbone.

2 Using a sharp knife, follow the contour of the breastbone to cut the flesh neatly off the bone.

Bone a leg

1 Place the leg skin-side down on a cutting board. Using a small, sharp knife, cut the flesh away from the thigh bone. Repeat on the drumstick.

2 Lift the bones up from the central knuckle joint. Using short strokes with the tip of your knife, remove the 2 bones from the flesh.

Bone a thigh

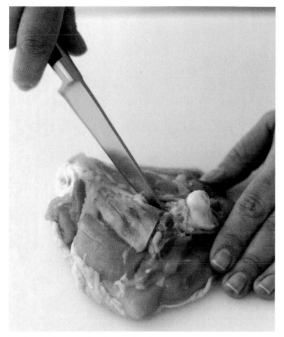

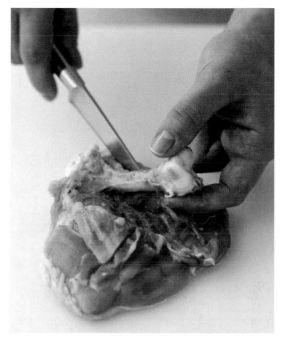

1 Place the thigh skin-side down on a cutting board. Using a small, sharp knife, cut away the flesh to expose the thigh bone.

2 Cut an incision through the flesh, following the contour of the exposed bone. Cut around the bone to cut it completely free from the flesh and discard and use for stock (see page 168).

Bone a drumstick

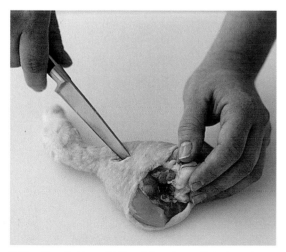

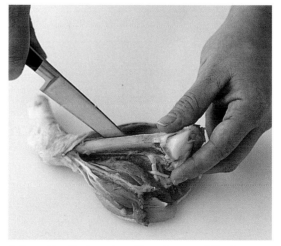

1 Starting in the middle of the drumstick, insert the tip of your knife until you locate the bone. Slice along the bone in both directions to expose it fully.

2 Open the flesh and neatly cut around the bone to free it completely from the flesh and discard, or use to flavour stock (see page 168).

Spatchcock

Ideal for grilling, this preparation method for small poultry flattens the bird to ensure even cooking. It is perfect if you want to cook poultry on a barbecue.

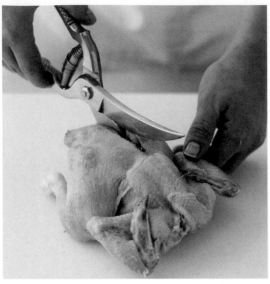

1 Place the bird breast-side down on a cutting board. Using poultry shears, cut along both sides of the backbone, remove it completely, and discard or use for stock. Open the bird and turn it over.

2 Using the heel of one hand and the other hand to stabilize, press firmly to crush the breastbone. Once flattened, use a sharp knife to cut slits into the legs and thighs to ensure even cooking.

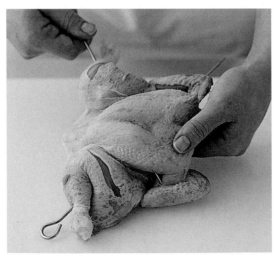

3 Carefully push one metal skewer diagonally through the left leg to the right wing, then another skewer through the right leg to the left wing.

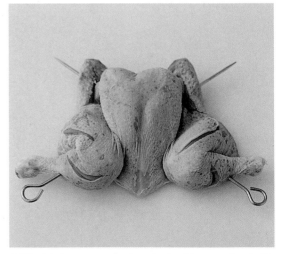

4 The bird can now be brushed with a marinade if desired, then grilled or roasted in the oven. Remove the skewers and carve the bird before serving.

Marinate

Using a marinade will produce more tender and flavourful poultry.

Mix the ingredients of your marinade in a bowl. In a separate large bowl, place the chicken pieces without overlapping them and coat with the marinade, turning the pieces to coat the other side. Cover the bowl with cling film and chill in the refrigerator for an hour, or more, depending on the marinade and the time available.

Stuff a chicken breast

Don't overstuff the chicken breasts – this will increase the risk of leakage.

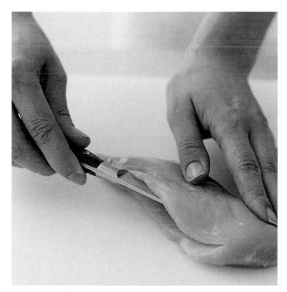

1 Using a sharp knife, cut a pocket about 4cm (1$^{1}/_{2}$in) deep into the side of the breast fillet. Make your cut so that both sides of the pocket are of even thickness, which will ensure even cooking.

2 Gently press the filling into the pocket and close the flesh back together. Secure with a cocktail stick. Rolling the stuffed fillet in a crumb coating before cooking will help seal the pocket.

Steeping

The meat produced by steeping is popular in Chinese cooking. First, simmer your chicken in stock or water, then remove from the heat. As the water cools, the meat gently cooks and becomes extremely tender.

1 Choose between either stock or water to steep your chicken. Place the bird in a large pot and cover with the liquid.

2 Add some spring onions, bring to the boil, cover with a tight-fitting lid and simmer for 20 minutes. Remove the pot from the heat and leave for around 1 hour with the lid still tightly fitted.

3 Remove the chicken from the pot and pierce the thickest part of the leg. If the juices run clear, the chicken is cooked. Place into a large bowl of iced cold water. Leave until completely cool.

4 Remove the chicken from the water and drain well. Place the bird on a cutting board and carve according to your recipe.

Poaching

Don't allow the liquid to boil, keep it simmering for delicate meat. Try adding some vegetables to the pot too to make a roast with a difference.

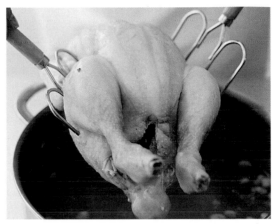

1 Place your chicken in a pan and add water until just covered. Remove the chicken and bring the water to the boil. Add a pinch of salt and replace the chicken, cover, and leave to simmer for 35 minutes.

2 The bird is cooked when the juices run clear when the leg is skewered in its thickest part. If the juices are red, return to the pan for another 10 minutes. Remove the bird from the pan and carve.

Braising and pot-roasting

The rich flavours produced by braising and pot-roasting chicken make them ideal techniques if you want to make a flavour-packed dish with minimal effort.

1 Joint a chicken into 8 pieces and season with salt and black pepper (see page 12). Heat around 30g (1oz) butter in a heavy saucepan and add the chicken. Turn the chicken and cook until golden.

2 Stir in 1 tbsp plain flour and cook for 2 minutes. Stir in 1 tbsp passata, 250ml (8fl oz) red wine, and 1 tbsp sugar, and bring to the boil. Turn the heat down, cover, and cook for 50 minutes or until cooked.

Roasting

This favourite technique takes minutes in preparation and, if you follow a few golden rules, you always achieve a fantastic result. For cooking times, see page 8.

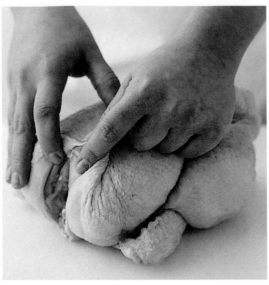

1 Put the raw bird on a large, clean cutting board and pull the skin back from around the neck cavity. Locate the wishbone with your finger and work it loose by gently moving your finger back and forth.

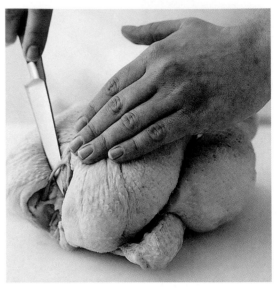

2 Insert a small, sharp knife behind the bone and work it down to the bottom of one of the wishbone's "arms", then cut it free from the flesh. In an older chicken the wishbone will be quite strong.

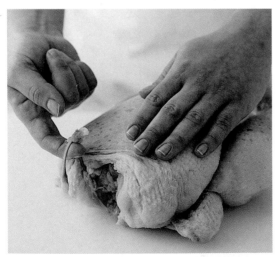

3 Pull the wishbone out by hooking your finger under the centre and gently tugging until it comes free. Removing the wishbone before roasting makes the bird easier to carve when serving.

4 Smear butter or rub oil all over the outside of the bird, then season well with salt and black pepper inside and out. (If you are stuffing the bird, push the stuffing under the breast skin.)

5 Put the bird in a roasting tin and place in a preheated oven. Baste regularly and turn it breast-side down after 30 minutes to baste the breast meat.

6 Turn the chicken breast-side up for the last 20 minutes. The bird is cooked when the juices run clear when the leg is skewered in its thickest part.

Add stuffing

1 In a bowl, blend together your stuffing ingredients; butter, an egg, fresh breadcrumbs, chopped parsley, and lemon zest are shown here. Season with salt and pepper.

2 Carefully ease the skin away from the breast and gently push the stuffing under the skin from the neck end. This ensures the stuffing cooks through.

Resting and carving

Leaving a roast to rest is very important. It allows the juices to flow to all parts of the bird so that every slice will be as tender as the last.

1 After roasting, transfer the bird to a cutting board, breast-side up, cover with foil, and leave to rest for 15 minutes in a warm place. This allows the juices to flow throughout the bird and keep the meat moist.

2 Remove the legs by cutting the skin between the leg and the body and pushing the blade down to where the leg bone joins the body. It is easiest if you angle the blade into the body slightly.

3 Work the blade from side to side to loosen the joint, then, with a slight sawing motion, push the blade through the joint, cutting the leg free. Transfer the leg to a warmed plate and repeat with the other leg.

4 Remove a breast by cutting as if you are dividing the bird in half, just to one side of the breastbone. As the blade hits the bone, cut along the bone; remove all the meat; repeat on the other side.

5 Place one breast cut-side down on the cutting board. Slice the breast horizontally, leaving the wing with a piece of breast meat attached.

6 Carve each leg by cutting it in half through the joint at the midway point. As you reach the joint, work the blade into the joint to separate the pieces.

Make gravy

1 Using a large spoon, skim off most the fat from the pan juices. Mix 1 tbsp plain white flour with 1 tbsp of the chicken fat.

2 Put the roasting tin over a low heat. Whisk in the fat mixture. Add 300ml (10fl oz) stock or water and bring to the boil, still whisking. Strain and serve hot.

Ready in 30 minutes Make these recipes in half an hour or under.

Chicken croustades page 44

Devilled turkey page 82

Chicken and noodle stir-fry
page 182

Smoked chicken and tarragon mousse page 50

Spicy turkey burgers page 88

Warm chicken salad page 180

Turkey à la king page 80

Chicken chow mein page 186

Thai green chicken curry page 70

Healthy These recipes are all low in fat or low GI.

Thai noodle stir-fry page 62

Chicken noodle soup page 178

Chicken cacciatore page 106

Roast chicken page 154

Chicken biryani page 132

Baked poussin with lemon and paprika page 118

Cock-a-leekie soup page 176

Chicken jalfrezi page 84

Rice porridge page 192

Roast turkey with cranberry pistachio stuffing page 164

Roast chicken with thyme and lemon page 158

Budget All use cheaper cuts of a bird or other cheap ingredients.

Southern fried chicken page 66

Chicken croustades page 44

Coronation chicken rolls
page 52

Honey mustard barbecued chicken page 54

Chicken chow mein page 186

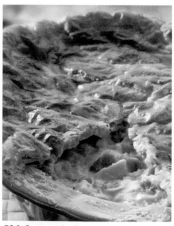

Chicken pot pie page 100

Cock-a-leekie soup page 176

Chicken croquettes page 184

Chicken jalousie page 190

Spicy turkey burgers page 88

Chicken korma page 104

Chicken tikka masala page 108

Tandoori chicken page 134

Calzone page 174

Chicken liver pâté page 40

Prepare ahead Make these dishes well before you plan to serve them.

Coarse meat terrine page 38

Chicken croquettes page 184

Turkey à la king page 80

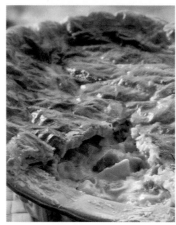

Chicken pot pie page 100

Chicken tikka masala page 108

Coq au vin page 112

Rice porridge page 192

Chicken liver pâté page 40

Duck confit page 116

Thai green chicken curry
page 70

Chicken jalfrezi page 84

Chicken and apricot tagine
page 102

Spicy If you fancy a curry or something with a kick, choose one of these.

Thai noodle stir-fry page 62

Devilled turkey page 82

Chicken tikka masala page 108

Couscous royale page 92

Chicken korma page 104

Chicken piri-piri page 94

Thai green chicken curry
page 70

Chilli and orange duck page 142

Spicy turkey burgers page 88

Chicken biryani page 132

Chicken jalfrezi page 84

Jambalaya page 98

Poached guinea fowl with spiced lentils page 138

Light For lunches, snacks, and light suppers, choose one of these tasty bites.

Warm chicken salad page 180

Chicken satay page 48

Cock-a-leekie soup page 176

Chicken with herb sauce
page 78

Turkey milanese page 86

Chicken in balsamic vinegar page 124

Turkey kebabs page 58

Lemon honey chicken with mustard mayonnaise page 140

Smoked chicken and tarragon mousse page 50

Chicken and noodle stir-fry page 182

Chicken croustades page 44

Chicken wrapped in pancetta and sage page 136

Saffron chicken brochettes page 56

EAT WITH YOUR FINGERS

Coarse meat terrine

Full of rich flavour, this pâté is extremely versatile.

INGREDIENTS

350g (12oz) rindless streaky bacon rashers
250g (9oz) chicken livers
300g (10oz) minced pork
450g (1lb) minced veal
1 onion, finely chopped
2 garlic cloves, crushed
1 tsp dried oregano
$^{1}/_{2}$ tsp ground allspice
115g (4oz) butter, melted
120ml (4fl oz) dry sherry
salt and freshly ground black pepper

METHOD

1 Preheat the oven to 180°C (350°F/Gas 4). Using the back of a knife, stretch the bacon rashers, and use them to line the terrine dish, or other ovenproof bowl or dish, leaving the ends hanging over the sides of the dish.

2 Mince or chop the chicken livers and mix with the minced pork, minced veal, onion, garlic, oregano, allspice, and melted butter. Stir in the sherry and season with salt and pepper.

3 Spoon the mixture into the dish and fold the ends of the bacon over the top. Cover tightly with foil or a lid, and stand the dish in a roasting tin, filled with enough hot water to reach halfway up the sides of the terrine dish.

4 Cook in the oven for 1½ hours, then remove and cover with fresh foil. Place a weight on top and leave for up to 24 hours, then turn out and cut into slices.

GOOD WITH Slices of warm crusty bread or toast, topped with a gherkin or cocktail onion.

PREPARE AHEAD You can start this recipe the day before, as the longer the cooked terrine is pressed with a heavy weight, such as unopened cans, the better the flavour and texture will be.

serves 8

prep 30 mins,
plus pressing
• cook 1½ hrs

1.2 litre (2 pint)
terrine dish

freeze for up to
1 month

Chicken liver pâté

The red wine adds flavour to this spread and cuts through the richness of the liver.

INGREDIENTS

350g (12oz) chicken livers, thawed if frozen
115g (4oz) butter
¼ tsp dried thyme
150ml (5fl oz) red wine
10 chives, snipped
salt and freshly ground black pepper
sprigs of fresh thyme, to garnish

METHOD

1 Rinse the chicken livers and pat them dry with kitchen paper. Trim away any white sinew or greenish portions from the livers with small scissors, then cut each in half.

2 Melt half the butter in a large frying pan over a medium heat until it foams. Add the livers and cook, stirring often, for 4 minutes, or until browned.

3 Add the thyme, wine, and chives to the pan. Bring to the boil then reduce the heat and cook, stirring occasionally for 4 minutes, or until the liquid is reduced and the livers are just cooked through when sliced open.

4 Remove the pan from the heat and leave to cool for 10 minutes. Add salt and pepper to taste, then tip the livers and sauce into a blender, and blend until smooth. Adjust the seasoning if necessary. Spoon the pâté into a serving bowl, pressing it down with the back of the spoon so it is firmly packed, then set aside.

5 Melt the remaining butter over a medium heat, then pour it over the top of the pâté. Chill, uncovered, for at least 2 hours. Serve garnished with sprigs of fresh thyme.

GOOD WITH Toasted French bread slices or cornichons, which are the traditional French accompaniment.

PREPARE AHEAD This is best made 1 day and a maximum of 3 days in advance so the flavours have time to develop. Keep covered and chilled in the refrigerator.

serves 4

prep 10 mins,
plus cooling
and chilling
• cook 15 mins

freeze the livers
for up to
3 months
before using

Smoked chicken and spinach filo parcels

These little parcels are delicious served hot or cold.

INGREDIENTS
225g (8oz) fresh spinach
olive oil
4 spring onions, finely chopped
115g (4oz) smoked chicken
85g (3oz) crème fraîche
1 tbsp chopped tarragon
60g (2oz) pine nuts, toasted
1 tsp Dijon mustard
grated zest of 1 lemon
freshly ground black pepper
200g packet filo pastry
60g (2oz) butter, melted
30g (1oz) Parmesan cheese, grated

METHOD

1 Preheat the oven to 180°C (350°F/Gas 4). Wash the spinach, remove any tough stalks and wilt in a saucepan with a little olive oil. Drain well and cool. Place in a food processor with the spring onions, smoked chicken, crème fraîche, and tarragon, then process for a slightly chunky texture. The mixture should not be totally smooth. Add the pine nuts, mustard, and lemon zest. Season to taste with freshly ground black pepper.

2 Lay the filo pastry out on a clean surface. Cover with a clean, damp tea towel to stop the pastry drying out. Brush 1 strip of filo pastry with butter, then place another layer on top and brush with butter. Cut the pastry into 7.5cm (3in) strips, and place 1 rounded tsp of the spinach mixture near the top. Take the right corner and fold diagonally to the left to form a triangle over the filling. Fold along the crease of the triangle and repeat until you reach the end of the strip. Brush with butter once finished and scatter with Parmesan cheese. Place on a lined baking sheet.

3 Repeat with the rest of the pastry and filling to make 12 parcels. Bake for 20 minutes. Remove from the baking sheet and put on a wire rack to cool.

GOOD WITH Your choice of dipping sauce.

PREPARE AHEAD The pastry parcels can be made the day before and chilled in the refrigerator until ready to cook.

serves 6

prep 25 mins
• cook 20 mins

freeze,
unbaked, for
up to 1 month

Chicken croustades

Tarragon and chicken is a popular combination.

INGREDIENTS

1 skinless boneless chicken breast, cooked
2 tbsp mayonnaise
1 tsp chopped tarragon, plus
    12 leaves, to garnish
1 tsp wholegrain mustard
1 tsp lemon juice
salt and freshly ground black pepper
12 croustade baskets

METHOD

1 Shred the chicken into small pieces and set aside.

2 In a bowl, mix together the mayonnaise, tarragon, mustard, and lemon juice, and season to taste with salt and pepper. Add the chicken and stir until well combined.

3 Divide the mixture between the croustade baskets and garnish each one with a tarragon leaf. Serve within 1 hour of filling.

PREPARE AHEAD The chicken filling can be prepared several hours in advance, and chilled until needed.

serves 12

prep 15 mins

44

Buffalo chicken wings

Moreish, sticky charred chicken wings served with a rich blue cheese dip.

INGREDIENTS
2 tbsp olive oil, plus extra for oiling
1 shallot, finely chopped
1 garlic clove, crushed
2 tbsp tomato purée
1 tbsp dried oregano
few drops of Tabasco sauce
2 tsp light soft brown sugar
salt and freshly ground black pepper
12 chicken wings, tips removed

For the blue cheese dip
150ml (5fl oz) soured cream
75g (2$\frac{1}{2}$oz) blue cheese, such
   as Roquefort or Dolcelatte, crumbled
juice of $\frac{1}{2}$ lemon
2 tbsp finely snipped chives

METHOD
1 Place the olive oil, shallot, garlic, tomato purée, oregano, Tabasco, and sugar in a blender, season with salt and pepper, and process until smooth. Spoon into the large food bag, and add the chicken wings. Shake the bag until the meat is well coated with marinade. Chill for at least 30 minutes to marinate.

2 Preheat the oven to 180°C (350°F/Gas 4). Remove the chicken wings from the bag and lay them, skin-side down, on 2 lightly oiled baking sheets. Place in the oven and cook for 10 minutes. Turn the pieces over and cook for a further 15 minutes, or until cooked through.

3 Meanwhile, mix together all the ingredients for the blue cheese dip. Serve the chicken wings hot, with the dip on the side.

PREPARE AHEAD The chicken can be coated in the tomato mixture and left to marinate for a few hours until ready to cook.

serves 4

prep 20 mins,
plus marinating
• cook 25 mins

large plastic
food bag

EAT WITH YOUR FINGERS

Chicken satay

The authentic version is made with Indonesian soy sauce, kecap manis, but Chinese or Japanese soy can also be used.

INGREDIENTS

3 skinless boneless chicken breasts
1/2 tsp salt
2cm (3/4in) piece of fresh root ginger,
  peeled and grated
2 garlic cloves, crushed
1/2 tsp ground cumin
2 tsp ground coriander
1 tsp lemongrass purée
4 tsp brown sugar
juice of 1/2 lime
2 tbsp kecap manis or soy sauce
vegetable oil

For the sauce
250g (9oz) peanut butter
2 garlic cloves, crushed
30g (1oz) creamed coconut,
  coarsely chopped
1 tbsp dark soy sauce
1 tbsp dark brown sugar
1cm (1/2in) piece of fresh root ginger,
  peeled and finely chopped
1 tbsp lemon juice
cayenne pepper
salt and freshly ground black pepper
lime wedges, to garnish

METHOD

1 Cut the chicken into thin strips across the grain of the meat. Spread them out in a shallow, non-metallic dish.

2 In a small bowl, mix together the salt, ginger, garlic, cumin, coriander, lemongrass purée, sugar, lime juice, kecap manis, and 2 tsp of the vegetable oil. Spoon this mixture over the chicken, turning the strips until they are well coated. Cover the dish with cling film and place in the refrigerator to marinate overnight.

3 To make the satay sauce, put the peanut butter with half the garlic in a small saucepan and cook over a low heat for 2 minutes. Add 175ml (6fl oz) water, the creamed coconut, soy sauce, sugar, and ginger, and cook for 2 minutes, stirring until smooth.

4 Add the lemon juice and remaining garlic and season to taste with cayenne pepper, salt, and pepper. Let the sauce cool, cover with cling film, and chill.

5 When ready to cook, remove the chicken from the dish and thread the pieces on to the wooden skewers. In a pan over low heat, re-heat the satay sauce, stirring frequently to prevent lumps.

6 Brush the chicken with oil and grill or barbecue for 5 minutes, turning over once, or until the chicken is cooked through. Garnish with lime wedges and serve hot with the satay sauce.

PREPARE AHEAD Complete steps 1 and 2 up to 24 hours in advance. The satay sauce can be made the day before and reheated.

serves 6

prep 20 mins,
plus marinating
• cook 5 mins

soak skewers
for 30 mins
before use

wooden
skewers

Smoked chicken and tarragon mousse

Quick, healthy, and impressive – chicory leaves are a great alternative to crackers or bread.

INGREDIENTS
225g (8oz) smoked chicken breasts
zest and juice of $\frac{1}{2}$ lemon
1 tbsp chopped fresh tarragon
3 tbsp mayonnaise
2 tbsp Dijon mustard
sea salt and freshly ground black pepper
1 head of red chicory
1 head of white chicory
chives, to garnish (optional)

METHOD
1 Remove any skin and bone from the smoked chicken and discard. Cut the meat into small pieces. Place the chicken in a food processor with the lemon zest and juice, tarragon, mayonnaise, and mustard. Process until finely chopped. Season to taste with salt and pepper.

2 To serve, separate the chicory leaves and trim, if necessary. Place teaspoonfuls of the mousse on to the stalk ends of the chicory leaves. Garnish with chives, if using.

PREPARE AHEAD You can make the mousse 1 day in advance and chill. Once placed on the chicory leaves, serve within 1 hour.

serves 10–12

prep 10 mins

Coronation chicken rolls

These rolls are synonymous with British summer picnics and garden parties.

INGREDIENTS

1 tbsp sunflower oil
1 shallot, finely chopped
1 tsp curry paste (either mild or hot,
    according to taste)
1 tbsp tomato purée
dash of Worcestershire sauce
115g (4oz) mayonnaise
6 apricot halves canned in fruit juice, drained
350g (12oz) cooked chicken, chopped
    or shredded into small bite-sized pieces
8 bridge rolls, split and spread with
    butter or left plain as preferred
2 tbsp chopped parsley

METHOD

1 Heat the oil in a small pan and fry the shallot until softened but not browned. Add the curry paste, cook for 1 minute over a low heat, and then stir in the tomato purée and Worcestershire sauce. Remove from the heat and set aside to cool.

2 Place the onion mixture, mayonnaise, and apricot halves in a food processor or blender and process until smooth and creamy. Transfer to a bowl and stir in the chicken. Cover and chill until needed.

3 To serve, pile on to the bridge rolls and sprinkle with the chopped fresh parsley.

PREPARE AHEAD The filling can be made 1 day in advance, then spooned on to the bridge rolls up to 1–2 hours before serving.

serves 4

**prep 15 mins,
plus cooling
• cook 5 mins**

Honey mustard barbecued chicken

The sweetness of honey and the tang of wholegrain mustard make a delicious glaze for barbecued chicken.

INGREDIENTS

8 chicken drumsticks or thighs
120ml (4fl oz) tomato ketchup
2 tbsp olive oil
120ml (4fl oz) orange juice
60ml (2fl oz) balsamic vinegar
1 tsp dried oregano
1/4 tsp freshly ground black pepper
1 garlic clove, crushed

For the glaze

2 tbsp clear honey
2 tbsp wholegrain mustard
zest of 1 lemon

METHOD

1 Make 2 or 3 cuts into each chicken portion and place in a large bowl. Make the marinade by putting the tomato ketchup, olive oil, orange juice, vinegar, oregano, pepper, and garlic into the bowl and whisking together with a fork until well mixed. Pour the marinade over the chicken, and turn the pieces to coat evenly. Refrigerate for at least 6 hours, or overnight if possible, turning the chicken occasionally.

2 Preheat the barbecue or grill to medium. Remove the chicken from the marinade, reserving it for basting. Barbecue over a medium-low heat for 15 minutes, turning once, and basting frequently with the reserved marinade.

3 Combine the honey, mustard, and zest to make the glaze, and brush the chicken. Cook for a further 10–15 minutes, turning, or until browned and cooked through. To test if the chicken is cooked, the juices should run clear and the meat should no longer be pink in the centre when a knife or skewer is inserted.

PREPARE AHEAD You can marinate the chicken for up to 24 hours.

serves 4

prep 10 mins,
plus marinating
• cook 30 mins

Saffron chicken brochettes

Ideal for a summer barbecue or as a bite-sized lunch.

INGREDIENTS
6 x 175g (6oz) skinless boneless chicken
  breasts, cubed
2 tbsp olive oil
zest and juice of 3 lemons
4 pinches of saffron powder, dissolved
  in 1 tbsp boiling water
salt and freshly ground black pepper
2 red onions, finely sliced
30g (1oz) butter
basil leaves, to garnish

METHOD
1 Put the chicken in a large bowl. Whisk together the oil, lemon zest, the juice from 2 lemons, and the saffron. Season to taste with salt and pepper. Add the sliced onions and pour over the chicken. Mix, cover, and chill for 2 hours or overnight.

2 When ready to cook, melt the butter in a small pan with the remaining lemon juice.

3 Preheat the grill to High. Remove the chicken from the marinade and thread on to the skewers. Place under the grill with the onions. Turn and brush with lemon butter. Arrange on a heated plate and serve hot, scattered with herbs.

serves 6

prep 10 mins,
plus marinating
• cook 10 mins

soak skewers
for 30 mins
before use

wooden
skewers

Turkey kebabs

Great tasting when cooked on a barbecue, you'll want to make these kebabs every week of the summer.

INGREDIENTS
60ml (2fl oz) light soy sauce
2 tbsp olive oil
2 garlic cloves, finely chopped
³/₄ tsp ground ginger
¹/₄ tsp chilli flakes
675g (1¹/₂lb) skinless boneless turkey breasts,
   cut into 2.5cm (1in) cubes
1 red pepper, deseeded and cut into
   2.5cm (1in) pieces
1 green pepper, deseeded and cut into
   2.5cm (1in) pieces
1 large courgette, cut into 2.5cm (1in) slices

For the dip
250ml (8fl oz) plain yogurt
2 tbsp mint, chopped
¹/₂ tsp ground cumin

METHOD
1 Combine the soy sauce, oil, garlic, ginger, and chilli. Add the turkey pieces and toss to coat. Cover, chill, and marinate for at least 1 hour.

2 Thread the turkey, peppers, and courgette onto the skewers and brush with any leftover marinade. Grill for 5–6 minutes on each side, or until cooked through.

3 Mix together the yogurt, mint, and cumin, and serve alongside.

makes 6

prep 20 mins,
plus marinating
• cook 10–12 mins

soak skewers
for 30 mins
before use

6 metal or
wooden
skewers

SIMPLE SUPPERS

Thai noodle stir-fry

A fragrant and colourful stir-fry with the flavours of Thailand.

INGREDIENTS

175g (6oz) thin rice noodles
1 stalk lemongrass
3 tbsp groundnut oil or vegetable oil
3 skinless boneless chicken breasts,
    cut into thin strips
1 onion, sliced
1 tsp finely grated root ginger
1 fresh red chilli, deseeded and
    finely chopped
1 orange pepper, deseeded and sliced
115g (4oz) shiitake mushrooms, sliced
2 heads of pak choi, shredded
2 tbsp light soy sauce
1 tbsp Thai fish sauce
1 tsp sweet chilli sauce

METHOD

1 Soak the noodles in a bowl of boiling water until softened, or as directed on the packet. Drain and set aside. Meanwhile, remove and discard the outer leaves of the lemongrass and trim away the tough woody end. Finely chop.

2 Heat 2 tbsp of the oil in a wok and stir-fry the chicken over a high heat for 2–3 minutes, or until lightly browned. Remove from the pan and set aside.

3 Reduce the heat to medium, add the remaining oil, and stir-fry the onion for 2 minutes. Add the lemongrass, ginger, chilli, orange pepper, and mushrooms, and stir-fry for 2 minutes.

4 Add the pak choi and stir-fry for a further 2 minutes, then return the chicken to the pan and add the noodles. Pour in the soy sauce, fish sauce, and sweet chilli sauce, and toss everything together over the heat for 2–3 minutes, or until piping hot and the chicken is cooked through. Serve at once.

serves 4

prep 20 mins
• cook 15 mins

low fat

Chicken kiev

This classic garlic- and butter-stuffed chicken dish makes a satisfying family supper. The breadcrumbed coating prevents the butter leaking out.

INGREDIENTS

100g (3^1/$_2$oz) butter, softened
2 garlic cloves, crushed
finely grated zest of 1 lemon
2 tbsp chopped parsley
salt and freshly ground black pepper
4 skinless boneless chicken breasts
3 tbsp plain flour
1 egg, beaten
150g (5^1/$_2$oz) fresh breadcrumbs
sunflower oil, for deep-frying

METHOD

1 Place the butter in a bowl and stir in the garlic, lemon zest, and parsley. Season to taste with salt and pepper. Form into a block, wrap in cling film, then chill until firm.

2 Place each chicken breast between 2 sheets of cling film; pound them flat using a rolling pin.

3 Cut the butter into 4 sticks and place one on each of the breasts. Fold the other side of the chicken up and over the butter, enclosing it completely.

4 Season the flour with salt and pepper. Keeping the chicken closed, dip each piece in the seasoned flour, then in the beaten egg, and finally into the breadcrumbs to coat evenly.

5 Heat the oil to 180°C (350°F). Fry the chicken for 6–8 minutes depending on size, or until golden brown.

6 Remove and drain on kitchen paper. Serve hot.

GOOD WITH A fresh mixed salad and sautéed potatoes.

PREPARE AHEAD The flavoured butter can be made up to 1 day in advance and chilled.

serves 4

prep 25 mins,
plus chilling
• cook 8–10
mins

Southern fried chicken

This is succulent comfort food from America's Deep South, with the traditional accompaniment of a smooth cream sauce.

INGREDIENTS
225g (8oz) plain flour
salt and freshly ground black pepper
1 tsp dried thyme
1 tsp Cajun seasoning
1 tsp sugar
4 chicken drumsticks
4 chicken thighs
1 egg, beaten
vegetable oil, for deep-frying

For the cream sauce
1$\frac{1}{2}$ tbsp plain flour
250ml (8fl oz) full-fat milk

METHOD
1 Put the first 5 ingredients in the plastic food bag, hold the top firmly together and shake well.

2 Add the chicken drumsticks and thighs to the bag one at a time and shake until coated.

3 Dip the pieces into the beaten egg, then repeat step 2. Lay the coated chicken on a plate in a single layer and chill for 30 minutes.

4 Heat the oil for deep-frying to 160°C (325°F) and fry the chicken for 15–20 minutes, or until golden brown and cooked through, then drain on kitchen paper.

5 To make the cream sauce, spoon 2 tbsp of the fryer oil into a saucepan and stir in the flour. Cook over a low heat for 1 minute, then gradually whisk in the milk and black pepper to taste. Stir over a low heat until thickened and smooth.

GOOD WITH Mashed potatoes and corn on the cob.

PREPARE AHEAD Steps 1 and 2 can be completed 1 hour or more before cooking.

serves 4

prep 20 mins,
plus chilling
• cook 25 mins

plastic food
bag, deep-fat
fryer or large
deep saucepan
half-filled
with oil

Chicken in garlic sauce

Don't be put off by the large quantity of garlic, as the flavour will mellow in the cooking.

INGREDIENTS

15 garlic cloves, unpeeled
salt and freshly ground black pepper
2 tbsp olive oil
30g (1oz) unsalted butter
4 chicken breasts, skin on
1 bay leaf
450ml (15fl oz) dry cider
200ml (7fl oz) apple juice
200ml (7fl oz) double cream
1 tbsp thyme leaves

METHOD

1 Preheat the oven to 180°C (350°F/Gas 4). Cook the whole, unpeeled garlic cloves in a pan of boiling salted water for 4 minutes. Drain, cool slightly, then peel and set aside.

2 Heat the oil and butter in the casserole. When sizzling, add the chicken, skin-side down, and cook for 4–5 minutes, or until deep golden brown. Turn the chicken over and add the garlic cloves, bay leaf, cider, and apple juice. Cover and transfer to the oven for 20–25 minutes, or until the chicken is cooked through.

3 Lift the chicken out of the pan. Remove half the garlic cloves and discard. Bring the remaining juices up to the boil. Crush the garlic into the juices with a fork, then boil until reduced and thickened slightly.

4 Add the cream, season to taste with salt and pepper, and simmer for 1 minute. Return the chicken to the sauce and baste with the juices; add the thyme leaves and serve immediately.

GOOD WITH Boiled new potatoes and green beans.

serves 4

prep 10 mins
• cook 40 mins

shallow
flameproof
casserole

freeze, without
the cream and
thyme, for
up to 3 months

Thai green chicken curry

By using a shop-bought jar of Thai curry paste, this flavoursome dish is very quick to prepare.

INGREDIENTS
1 tbsp olive oil
4 tsp shop-bought Thai red curry paste
   or green curry paste (use more
   paste for a spicier sauce)
4 skinless boneless chicken breasts,
   about 140g (5oz) each, cut into
   bite-sized pieces
2 tbsp light soy sauce
400ml can coconut milk
175g (6oz) open-cap mushrooms, chopped
6 spring onions, trimmed, with the green
   part cut into 5mm ($^1/_4$in) slices
salt and freshly ground black pepper
chopped coriander, to garnish

METHOD
1 Heat the oil in a large frying pan over a medium heat. Add the curry paste and stir. Add the chicken and stir-fry for 2 minutes, or until lightly browned.

2 Pour in the soy sauce and coconut milk and bring to the boil, stirring. Lower the heat, stir in the mushrooms and most of the spring onions, and season with salt and pepper to taste, then simmer for about 8 minutes, or until the chicken is tender and cooked through.

3 Serve hot, garnished with coriander, and the remaining sliced spring onions.

GOOD WITH Boiled or steamed long-grain rice or plain noodles, as a starter or part of a Thai buffet.

PREPARE AHEAD Complete up to 24 hours in advance and reheat.

serves 4

prep 10 mins
• cook 10 mins

Chicken schnitzels

This quick dish is suitable for a family supper or a dinner party.

INGREDIENTS

45g (1$\frac{1}{2}$oz) plain flour
1 egg, beaten
about 60g (2oz) fine breadcrumbs
4 skinless boneless chicken breasts
salt and freshly ground black pepper
6 tbsp rapeseed oil
2 lemons, cut in half, to serve

METHOD

1 Put the flour in a shallow bowl, the egg in another bowl, and the breadcrumbs in a third bowl, set aside.

2 Put the chicken breasts, and the thin, small fillets, if attached, between 2 sheets of greaseproof paper and pound with a rolling pin until they are very thin. Season to taste with salt and pepper.

3 Coat the chicken in the flour, then in the beaten egg, and then in the breadcrumbs, pressing them evenly on to both sides. Place on a baking sheet or plate in one layer and chill in the refrigerator, uncovered, for at least 30 minutes.

4 Heat 3 tbsp of the oil in a non-stick frying pan over a medium-high heat. Add 2 of the schnitzels and fry for 3 minutes on each side, or until golden brown and cooked through. Drain on kitchen paper and keep hot.

5 Add the remaining oil to the pan, and fry the remaining schnitzels, as before.

6 Serve immediately, garnished with lemon halves, for squeezing over the schnitzels.

GOOD WITH Sautéed potatoes and green beans, or served cold, cut into slices, with potato salad.

PREPARE AHEAD The chicken can be prepared up to step 3, then covered and chilled for up to 8 hours.

serves 4

prep 10 mins,
plus chilling
• cook 12 mins

freeze for up to
3 months;
thaw at room
temperature,
then reheat

Seared herbed chicken with green herb sauce

The herbed crust seals in the juices, keeping the meat succulent.

INGREDIENTS

6 skinless boneless chicken breasts,
  about 175g (6oz) each
2 tbsp plain flour
350g (12oz) breadcrumbs
2 tbsp chopped thyme
2 tbsp chopped parsley
175g (6oz) Parmesan cheese, finely grated
2 eggs, lightly beaten
4 tbsp olive oil
4 tbsp sunflower oil

For the green herb sauce

2 tbsp white wine vinegar
2 egg yolks
1 egg
1 tbsp Dijon mustard
1 tbsp soft brown sugar or caster sugar
300ml (10fl oz) sunflower oil
20g (³/₄oz) mixed herbs, such as parsley,
  basil, dill, watercress, coriander,
  and chives, roughly chopped
salt and freshly ground black pepper

METHOD

1 For the sauce, place the vinegar, yolks, egg, mustard, and sugar into a food processor or blender, then gradually add the oil with the motor running to form a thick and creamy mayonnaise. Once all the oil has been added, blend in the herbs. Season to taste with salt and pepper and set aside.

2 Cut the chicken into halves and dust lightly with flour. Place the breadcrumbs in a bowl with the thyme, parsley, and Parmesan, season to taste with salt and pepper, and mix well. Coat the chicken in the egg, then the breadcrumbs.

3 Heat the frying pan with some of each oil. Fry the chicken in 2–3 batches for 5 minutes on each side, or until crisp and golden, adding more oil with each batch. Drain, then serve with the green herb sauce.

serves 6

prep 20 mins
• cook 20–30 mins

freeze for up to
2 months

74

Sweet and sour chicken

This classic dish from Hong Kong is popular in Cantonese restaurants around the world.

INGREDIENTS

vegetable oil, for deep-frying and stir-frying
4 skinless boneless chicken breasts,
　cut into 2.5cm (1in) pieces
flour, to dust
2 tbsp unsalted cashew nuts
　or whole blanched almonds
1/2 red pepper, deseeded and chopped
8 spring onions, cut into 2.5cm (1in) pieces
1 pineapple ring, cut into chunks

For the batter

115g (4oz) self-raising flour
pinch of salt
1/2 tsp baking powder
250ml (8fl oz) lager

For the sauce

120ml (4fl oz) chicken stock
3 tbsp light soy sauce
1 tbsp clear honey
3 tbsp rice vinegar
2 tbsp tomato ketchup
2cm (3/4in) piece of fresh root ginger,
　peeled and grated
1 tsp cornflour

METHOD

1 To make the batter, sift the flour, the salt, and the baking powder into a large bowl. Make a well in the centre and add half the lager. Gradually combine, then whisk in the rest of the lager to make a smooth batter. Set aside for 30 minutes.

2 To make the sauce, put all the ingredients, except the cornflour, in a pan and stir over a low heat until the honey melts. Mix the cornflour with a little cold water until smooth, then add to the pan and stir until thickened and smooth. Simmer for 1 minute, then set aside. Preheat the oven to 130°C (250°F/Gas 1/2).

3 Heat the oil for deep-frying to 180°C (350°F). Dust the chicken pieces with flour, coat in the batter and deep-fry in batches for 3–4 minutes, or until golden brown and crisp. Drain and keep warm, uncovered, in the oven.

4 Heat 2 tbsp oil in the wok, add the nuts, and stir-fry for 30 seconds, or until golden. Remove and set aside to drain on kitchen paper. Add the red pepper and stir-fry for 3 minutes, then add the spring onions and pineapple, and stir-fry for 1 minute.

5 Pour the sauce into the wok, add the chicken, stir until coated, and simmer for 2 minutes. Serve immediately, scattered with the nuts.

PREPARE AHEAD Steps 1 and 2 can be completed several hours in advance.

serves 4

prep 30 mins,
plus standing
• cook 25 mins

deep-fat
fryer or large
deep saucepan
half-filled with
oil, wok

Chicken with herb sauce

This punchy sauce for chicken is easy to make – just whiz all the ingredients in a food processor.

INGREDIENTS

4 skinless boneless chicken breasts,
   about 175g (6oz) each
1 small onion, sliced
1 carrot, chopped
1 celery stick, chopped
few sprigs of parsley

For the sauce

60g (2oz) parsley
60g (2oz) basil
1 garlic clove
2 anchovies
1 tbsp capers, rinsed
1 tbsp red wine vinegar
salt and freshly ground black pepper
120ml (4fl oz) olive oil

METHOD

1 Preheat the oven to 190°C (375°F/Gas 5). Place the chicken in a roasting tin, add the vegetables, parsley, and enough water to cover. Cover the tin with foil and bake for 30 minutes. Remove from the oven and leave to cool in the liquid.

2 Make the sauce by placing all the ingredients, except the olive oil, into a food processor, process briefly, then, with the motor running, slowly pour in the olive oil.

3 To serve, slice the chicken thinly and discard the liquid. Spoon the sauce over the sliced chicken breasts and serve with the roasted vegetables.

GOOD WITH A selection of roasted vegetables, such as artichokes.

serves 4

prep 10 mins
• cook 30 mins

Turkey à la king

This dish is very easy to make and the paprika adds a rich spiciness.

INGREDIENTS

2 tbsp sunflower oil
60g (2oz) butter
1 onion, finely sliced
1 green pepper, deseeded and chopped
1 red pepper, deseeded and chopped
175g (6oz) mushrooms, sliced
30g (1oz) plain flour
1 tsp paprika
salt and freshly ground black pepper
450ml (15fl oz) milk
500g (1lb 2oz) cooked turkey,
    cut into bite-sized pieces

METHOD

1 Heat the oil and butter in a large pan and fry the onion gently until softened. Add the peppers and fry for 5 minutes.

2 Stir in the mushrooms and fry for 5 minutes, or until the peppers and mushrooms have softened slightly.

3 Sprinkle in the flour and paprika, season to taste with salt and pepper, and take the pan off the heat. Gradually blend in the milk, return the pan to a low heat, and stir until the sauce comes to the boil and is thickened and smooth.

4 Stir in the turkey and simmer, stirring occasionally, for 5 minutes, or until the turkey is heated through, and serve.

PREPARE AHEAD The dish can be prepared up to 24 hours in advance and reheated thoroughly when ready to serve.

serves 4

**prep 15 mins
• cook 15 mins**

**freeze for up to
3 months; thaw
completely
before
reheating**

Devilled turkey

Serve these spicy stir-fried turkey strips as a healthy lunch or supper.

INGREDIENTS

2 tbsp wholegrain mustard
2 tbsp mango chutney
2 tbsp Worcestershire sauce
$\frac{1}{4}$ tsp ground paprika
3 tbsp orange juice
1 red chilli, chopped (optional)
2 tbsp olive oil
450g (1lb) turkey breast escalope,
    cut into strips
1 onion, peeled and finely chopped
1 red pepper, cored and cut into strips
1 orange pepper, cored and cut into strips
1 garlic clove, crushed

METHOD

1 Mix the mustard, chutney, Worcestershire sauce, paprika, orange juice, and chilli, if using, together until well combined.

2 Heat the oil in a frying pan or wok, add the turkey, and cook over a high heat until browned. Remove the turkey from the pan and set aside, covered to keep it warm.

3 Add the onion to the pan and fry for 2–3 minutes, or until beginning to colour. Add the peppers and garlic and fry, stirring constantly, for 3–4 minutes, or until tender.

4 Stir in the mustard mixture and return the turkey to the pan. Cook for 5 minutes or until piping hot and the turkey is cooked through.

GOOD WITH Stir-fried spinach and rice or noodles.

serves 4

prep 10 mins
• cook 15 mins

Chicken jalfrezi

A spicy dish, with chillies and mustard seeds, for those who like their curries hot.

INGREDIENTS

2 tbsp sunflower oil
2 tsp ground cumin
2 tsp yellow mustard seeds
1 tsp ground turmeric
1 tbsp masala curry paste
2.5cm (1in) piece fresh root ginger,
   peeled and finely chopped
3 garlic cloves, crushed
1 onion, sliced
1 red pepper, deseeded and sliced
$1/2$ green pepper, deseeded and sliced
2 green chillies, deseeded and finely chopped
675g ($1^{1}/_{2}$lb) boneless chicken thighs or breasts,
   skinned and cut into 2.5cm (1in) pieces
225g can chopped tomatoes
3 tbsp chopped coriander

METHOD

1 Heat the oil in a large pan over a medium heat, add the cumin, mustard seeds, turmeric, and curry paste, and stir-fry for 1–2 minutes.

2 Add the ginger, garlic, and onion and fry, stirring frequently, until the onion starts to soften. Add the red and green peppers and the chillies and fry for 5 minutes.

3 Increase the heat to medium-high, add the chicken, and fry until starting to brown. Add the tomatoes and coriander, reduce the heat, and simmer for 10 minutes, or until the chicken is cooked through, stirring often. Serve hot.

GOOD WITH Basmati rice and poppadums.

PREPARE AHEAD The curry can be made up to 2 days in advance, chilled, and reheated to serve.

serves 4

prep 20 mins
• cook 25 mins

low fat

freeze for up to
3 months

Turkey milanese

Inspired by the classic veal dish, this features coated cutlets topped with a tomato and artichoke sauce.

INGREDIENTS

4 tbsp plain flour
salt and freshly ground black pepper
4 turkey breast cutlets, about 115g (4oz) each
3 tbsp olive oil
1 small onion, chopped
60ml (2fl oz) dry white wine
200g jar marinated artichoke hearts, drained
175g (6oz) can plum tomatoes, drained weight
few basil leaves, torn

METHOD

1 Combine the flour and 1½ tsp each of salt and pepper on a plate. Dip the turkey in the seasoned flour until lightly coated all over, shaking off any excess.

2 Heat 1 tbsp of the oil in a large frying pan over a medium-high heat. Add 2 of the cutlets and fry, turning once, for 2–3 minutes on each side, or until golden brown and cooked through. Remove from the pan and keep warm. Heat another 1 tbsp of oil and repeat with the remaining 2 cutlets.

3 Add the remaining oil to the pan and fry the onion for 4–5 minutes, or until soft. Add the wine and bring the mixture to the boil, stirring often to loosen any brown bits from the bottom of the pan. Stir in the artichokes, tomatoes, and basil, and bring back to the boil. Pour over the cutlets to serve.

GOOD WITH Buttered tagliatelle or other fat pasta noodles.

serves 4

prep 10 mins
• cook 20–25 mins

Spicy turkey burgers

The epitome of fast food, these spicy burgers take no time to prepare and are an instant hearty supper.

INGREDIENTS
450g (1lb) minced turkey
2 tbsp finely chopped onion
2 tbsp chopped parsley
2 tsp Dijon mustard
2 garlic cloves, finely chopped
60g (2oz) fresh breadcrumbs
1 egg white
salt and freshly ground black pepper
1 tbsp vegetable oil
4 seeded buns
1 large ripe tomato, sliced
2 handfuls of shredded lettuce

METHOD
1 Mix the turkey, onion, parsley, mustard, garlic, breadcrumbs, and egg white in a bowl, and season to taste with salt and pepper. Form into 4 patties, each 1cm (^{1}/2in) thick.

2 Heat the oil in a large frying pan. Add the patties and fry for 3–4 minutes on each side, or until browned and cooked through. Meanwhile, toast the buns.

3 Place a turkey patty into each bun, with 1–2 tomato slices and some shredded lettuce.

GOOD WITH Chunky chips or pickles and potato crisps.

serves 4

prep 10 mins
• cook 6 mins

Lemon chicken, Chinese-style

This popular Cantonese dish from Hong Kong is something of a one-off, as lemons are rarely used in Chinese cooking.

INGREDIENTS

200g (7oz) self-raising flour
1/4 tsp bicarbonate of soda
vegetable oil, for deep-frying
4 skinless boneless chicken breasts

For the lemon sauce

30g (1oz) cornflour
120ml (4fl oz) fresh lemon juice
350ml (12fl oz) chicken stock
2 tbsp clear honey
4 tbsp soft light brown sugar
1cm (1/2in) piece of fresh root ginger,
   peeled and grated

METHOD

1 Sift the flour and bicarbonate of soda into a large bowl, add 300ml (10fl oz) of cold water, and whisk to make a smooth batter. Set aside for 30 minutes.

2 Heat the oil for deep-frying to 180°C (350°F). Coat the chicken in the batter, then deep-fry in batches for 5 minutes, or until golden. Drain on kitchen paper.

3 Meanwhile, make the sauce by whisking the cornflour with the lemon juice to make a smooth paste. Pour this into a small saucepan and add the stock, honey, sugar, and ginger. Stir over a low heat until the sauce comes to the boil. Simmer for 1 minute, or until the sauce thickens.

4 Arrange the chicken on a serving platter and spoon the hot sauce over the top.

GOOD WITH Boiled rice and pak choi or steamed greens as a tasty lunch or supper dish, or as part of a larger Chinese-themed menu.

PREPARE AHEAD The batter can be made up to 2 hours in advance. Add a little water if it becomes too thick.

serves 4

**prep 20 mins,
plus standing
• cook 30 mins**

**deep-fat fryer
or large
saucepan**

Couscous royale

This richly spiced dish makes a colourful Moroccan feast.

INGREDIENTS

2 tbsp olive oil
600g (1lb 5oz) lean lamb leg, cut into chunks
6 chicken drumsticks and thighs
1 large red onion, sliced
2 garlic cloves, finely chopped
1 red pepper, deseeded and diced
1 aubergine, diced
4 tsp harissa paste
1 tbsp paprika
1 tsp ground turmeric
2 courgettes, sliced
200ml (7fl oz) chicken stock
400g can chickpeas, drained
400g can chopped tomatoes
175g (6oz) chorizo or cooked Merguez sausage, thickly sliced
salt and freshly ground black pepper
large sprig of fresh thyme
1 bay leaf
450g (1lb) couscous, cooked according
    to packet instructions
chopped coriander, to garnish

METHOD

1 Heat the oil in the casserole and brown the lamb and chicken in batches, turning occasionally. Remove from the pan and set aside to drain on kitchen paper.

2 Add the onion, garlic, pepper, and aubergine and fry, stirring, for 3–4 minutes. Stir in the harissa, paprika, and turmeric, and cook for a further 1 minute.

3 Add the lamb and chicken, courgettes, chicken stock, chickpeas, tomatoes, and chorizo, and season to taste with salt and pepper. Bring to the boil, then add the thyme and bay leaf, reduce the heat, cover tightly, and simmer gently over a low heat for 1 hour, or until the meats are tender.

4 Strain off the liquid, pour it into a wide pan, and bring to the boil, until slightly reduced.

5 Stir the meats and vegetables into the cooked couscous. Pour the reserved liquid over, and sprinkle with chopped coriander to serve.

PREPARE AHEAD You can prepare steps 1–4, then cool, and refrigerate. To serve, reheat with the cooking liquid until piping hot.

serves 6

prep 10 mins
• cook 1 hr
20 mins

large flameproof
casserole

freeze for up to
1 month

Chicken piri-piri

Piri-piri sauce is popular in Portugal and South Africa.

INGREDIENTS

1 chicken, about 1.5kg (3lb 3oz)
6 fresh red chillies or green chillies
3 garlic cloves
$\frac{1}{2}$ tsp dried oregano
2 tsp paprika
120ml (4fl oz) olive oil
4 tbsp red wine vinegar
1 tsp salt

METHOD

1 Preheat the oven to 190°C (375°F/Gas 5). Cut through the breastbone of the chicken and open it out. Cut off and throw away the wing tips, neck, and parson's nose.

2 Put the chillies on a baking sheet, roast for 15 minutes, then let cool.

3 Remove the stalks from the chillies and discard. Place the chillies with the rest of the ingredients in a pan, and cook over a low heat for 3–5 minutes, stirring frequently. Allow to cool, then blend to a purée.

4 Rub the mixture over the chicken, place in a non-metallic dish, cover, chill, and marinate for at least 1 hour.

5 Preheat the oven to 200°C (400°F/Gas 6). Roast the chicken for 45 minutes, turning once and basting frequently. Serve hot.

GOOD WITH Boiled or steamed rice, guacamole, and a simple salad.

serves 4

prep 20 mins,
plus cooling
and marinating
• cook 1 hr 15
mins

ONE-POT

Jambalaya

This one-pot meal captures authentic Creole and cajun flavours of Louisiana.

INGREDIENTS

60g (2oz) dripping or 4 tbsp sunflower oil

4 skinless boneless chicken thighs,
    cut into bite-sized pieces

225g (8oz) mix of garlic and spicy sausages
    (and smoked if liked), cut into thick slices

1 onion, finely chopped

2 garlic cloves, finely chopped

1 red pepper, deseeded and finely chopped

1 green pepper, deseeded and finely chopped

1 celery stick, thinly sliced

1 Scotch bonnet chilli, deseeded and chopped
    (leave the seeds in if you like your dish very hot)

350g (12oz) long-grain rice

1 tsp chilli powder

1 tsp Worcestershire sauce

2 tbsp tomato purée

2 bay leaves

2 tsp dried thyme

1 tsp salt

$\frac{1}{2}$ tsp smoked paprika

pinch of sugar

freshly ground black pepper

400g can chopped tomatoes

600ml (1 pint) chicken stock,
    vegetable stock, or water

12 large raw prawns, heads and
    tails removed and deveined

hot pepper sauce, to serve

METHOD

1 Melt half the dripping in the casserole over a high heat. Add the chicken pieces and fry, stirring occasionally, for 10 minutes, or until browned and the juices run clear. Remove with a slotted spoon and set aside on to kitchen paper.

2 Add the remaining dripping to the pan and heat. Add the sausages but not smoked sausages (if using), and fry, stirring occasionally, for 5 minutes, or until browned. Remove with a slotted spoon and set aside with the chicken.

3 Add the onion, garlic, peppers, celery, and chilli to the pan and fry for 5 minutes, or until softened, stirring frequently. Add the rice, and chilli powder, and cook, stirring for 1–2 minutes. Add the Worcestershire sauce and tomato purée, and cook, stirring for a further minute.

4 Return the chicken to the casserole, along with all the sausages, including smoked (if using), bay leaves, thyme, salt, paprika, and sugar, and season to taste with pepper. Pour in the tomatoes with their juice and the stock, and bring to the boil, stirring. Reduce the heat to a low heat, cover, and simmer for 12–15 minutes, or until the peppers are tender.

5 Add the prawns, and simmer covered, for 3–5 minutes, or until the prawns are pink. The rice should be tender and the mixture a little soupy. Transfer to a serving bowl. Serve with the hot pepper sauce alongside.

GOOD WITH Rustic bread to mop up the juices.

serves 4-6

prep 30 mins
• cook 45 mins

**large flameproof
casserole**

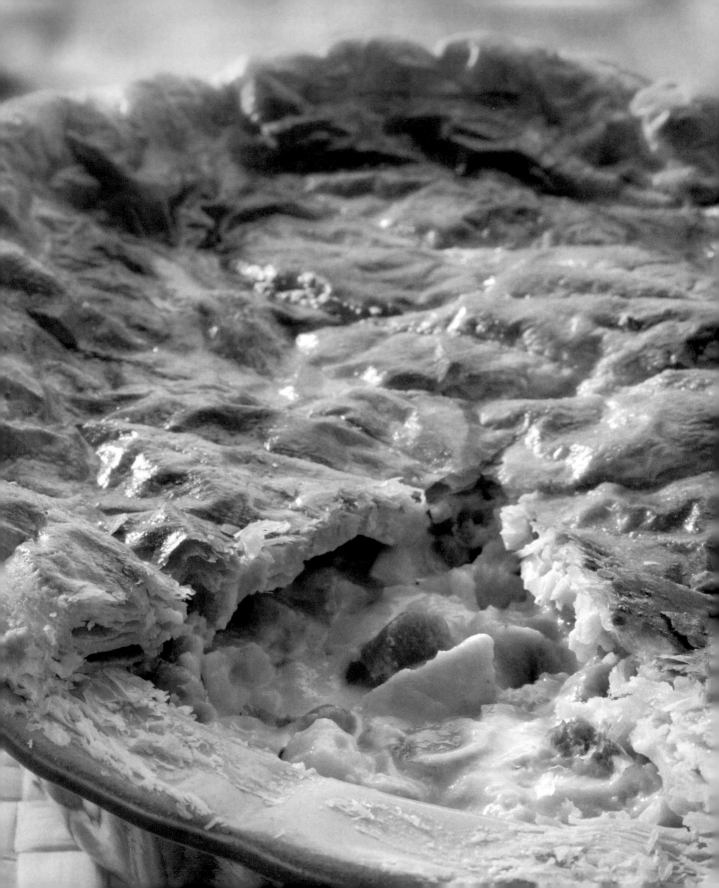

Chicken pot pie

This is a great recipe for transforming leftover roast chicken into a satisfying family meal.

INGREDIENTS
2 carrots, sliced
2 parsnips, peeled and sliced
600ml (1 pint) hot chicken stock
30g (1oz) butter
1 onion, finely chopped
2 celery stalks, roughly chopped
20g ($^3/_4$oz) plain flour
300g (10oz) frozen peas, thawed
$^1/_4$–$^1/_2$ tsp mustard powder
salt and freshly ground black pepper
350g (12oz) skinless boneless cooked
   chicken, cubed
250ml (8fl oz) double cream
250g (9oz) frozen puff pastry, thawed
1 small egg, beaten, to glaze

METHOD
1 Preheat the oven to 200°C (400°F/Gas 6). Put the carrots, parsnips, and stock in a large saucepan over a high heat and bring to the boil, then boil for 5 minutes or until the vegetables are just tender. Drain and reserve the stock.

2 Melt the butter in another pan over a medium heat. Add the onion and celery and fry, stirring frequently, for 5 minutes, or until softened. Add the flour and continue stirring for 2 minutes.

3 Gradually stir in the stock and bring to the boil, stirring. Reduce the heat and simmer for 2 minutes. Stir in the peas, the mustard, and salt and pepper to taste. Leave the mixture to cool, then stir in the root vegetables, chicken, and cream. Pour into a 1.5 litre (2$^3/_4$ pint) pie dish or ovenproof serving dish.

4 Roll out the pastry on a lightly floured surface until about $^1/_2$cm ($^1/_4$in) thick. Cut out a piece of pastry slightly larger than the dish. Brush the rim with water, then position the pastry over the filling and fold over the excess to make a stand-up edge. Crimp the edge, glaze the top with the beaten egg, and cut a small hole in the top to allow steam to escape.

5 Place the pie on a baking sheet and bake for 20 minutes, or until the pastry is puffed and golden and the filling is hot. Leave to stand for a few minutes, then serve.

GOOD WITH Steamed broccoli and, for heartier appetites, some boiled new potatoes.

PREPARE AHEAD The pie can be assembled a day in advance, refrigerated then baked.

serves 4

prep 15 mins
• cook 20 mins

pie dish or
ovenproof serving
dish with flat rim

freeze the pie
filling after step 3,
once cooled
completely, for
up to 3 months;
do not refreeze
if the chicken
has previously
been frozen

Chicken and apricot tagine

The dried fruit and warm spices in this dish are the unmistakable flavours of the Middle East.

INGREDIENTS

2 tbsp sunflower oil
1 onion, finely chopped
1 garlic clove, finely chopped
1 tsp ground ginger
1 tsp ground cumin
1 tsp turmeric
pinch of ground cinnamon
pinch of dried chilli flakes (optional)
1 tbsp tomato purée
600ml (1 pint) chicken stock
4 tbsp fresh orange juice
250g (9oz) mixed dried fruit, such as apricots
   and raisins
salt and freshly ground black pepper
675g (1¹/₂lb) skinless boneless chicken breasts
   and thighs, cut into large chunks
2 tbsp chopped coriander, to garnish

METHOD

1 Heat the oil in the casserole over a medium heat. Add the onion, garlic, ground spices, and chilli flakes, if using, and fry, stirring, for 5 minutes, or until the onions have softened. Stir in the tomato purée and stock and bring to the boil, stirring.

2 Add the orange juice, dried fruits, and salt and pepper to taste. Reduce the heat, partially cover the pan, and simmer for 15 minutes, or until the fruits are soft and the juices have reduced slightly.

3 Add the chicken, re-cover the casserole, and continue simmering for 20 minutes, or until the chicken is tender and the juices run clear. Adjust the seasoning, if necessary, then garnish with coriander and serve hot.

GOOD WITH Couscous.

PREPARE AHEAD The tagine can be cooked in advance, left to cool, and refrigerated for up to 2 days; reheat gently but thoroughly.

serves 4

prep 15 mins
• cook 35–40 mins

large flameproof
casserole

Chicken korma

A mild curry popular in Indian restaurants, this is a fragrant and aromatic dish with a creamy sauce.

INGREDIENTS

4 tbsp vegetable oil or ghee
8 skinless boneless chicken thighs,
    cut into 2$\frac{1}{2}$cm (1in) pieces
2 large onions, thinly sliced
1 tbsp ground coriander
1 tbsp ground cumin
1 tsp ground turmeric
$\frac{1}{2}$ tsp ground ginger
1 tsp chilli powder
1 tsp ground cardamom
2 garlic cloves, crushed
150g (5$\frac{1}{2}$oz) thick plain yogurt
1 tbsp plain flour
300ml (10fl oz) chicken stock
150ml (5fl oz) double cream
1 tbsp lemon juice

METHOD

1 Heat half of the oil in a large pan and fry the chicken in batches over a high heat until lightly browned on both sides. Remove from the pan and set aside.

2 Lower the heat, add the rest of the oil to the pan, and fry the onions until soft and golden. Add the spices and garlic and fry for 2 minutes, stirring occasionally.

3 Gradually stir in the yogurt. Put the flour in a small bowl, add a little stock and mix to a smooth paste. Pour the paste into the pan with the rest of the stock and bring to the boil, stirring constantly, then lower the heat. Return the chicken to the pan and simmer gently, for 15 minutes, or until cooked through, stirring occasionally.

4 Stir in the cream and lemon juice and simmer for a further 5 minutes before serving.

GOOD WITH Herb-flecked boiled rice, naan bread, and a variety of chutneys.

serves 4

prep 20 mins
• cook 45 mins

freeze for up to
1 month

104

Chicken cacciatore

This Italian dish translates as "hunter-style chicken", and is traditionally served with polenta to soak up the delicious juices.

INGREDIENTS
4 chicken legs, about 1.5kg
  (3lb 3oz) total weight
salt and freshly ground black pepper
2 tbsp olive oil
2 garlic cloves, sliced
1 medium onion, chopped
200ml (7fl oz) dry white wine
1 celery stalk, chopped
200g (7oz) button mushrooms, sliced
400g can chopped tomatoes
150ml (5fl oz) chicken stock
1 tbsp tomato purée
2 tsp chopped rosemary
2 tsp chopped sage
8 pitted black olives, halved

METHOD
1 Trim any excess fat from the chicken and season with salt and pepper. Heat half the oil in the casserole and fry the chicken in batches, until brown on all sides. Remove and keep hot. Pour the excess fat out of the pan.

2 Add the remaining oil, garlic, and onion and fry gently for 3–4 minutes, to soften but not brown. Add the wine and boil for 1 minute. Stir in the celery, mushrooms, tomatoes, stock, tomato purée, rosemary, and sage.

3 Return the chicken to the pan, cover, and cook over a low heat for 30 minutes, or until the chicken is cooked through.

4 Remove the lid, add the olives, then cover and cook for a further 5–10 minutes. Serve hot.

GOOD WITH Soft polenta and a side salad of fresh mixed leaves.

serves 4

prep 20 mins
•cook 35-40 mins

low fat

flameproof
casserole

Chicken tikka masala

An Indian restaurant dish, made popular in Britain.

INGREDIENTS
8 skinless boneless chicken thighs
2 garlic cloves, coarsely chopped
2.5cm (1in) piece of fresh root ginger,
   coarsely chopped
juice of 1 lime
1 red chilli, deseeded
2 tbsp coarsely chopped coriander leaves,
   plus extra to garnish
2 tbsp vegetable oil
1 red onion, chopped
1 tsp ground turmeric
1 tsp ground cumin
1 tbsp tomato purée
300ml (10fl oz) double cream
1 tbsp lemon juice
salt and freshly ground black pepper

METHOD
1 Place the chicken in a single layer in a shallow dish. Put the next 5 ingredients and 1 tbsp of the oil in a food processor, process into a paste, and spread over the chicken. Set aside to marinate for 2 hours.

2 Heat the remaining oil in a frying pan, add the onion, and fry until softened and starting to colour. Add the turmeric and cumin and fry gently for 2–3 minutes.

3 Preheat the grill on its highest setting. Lift the chicken from the dish, reserving any marinade left behind, and place on a foil-lined grill rack. Grill for 5 minutes, or until almost cooked and slightly scorched at the edges, turning once.

4 Stir the tomato purée and cream into the frying pan with any leftover marinade. Add the lemon and stir over a medium heat until mixed in. Place the chicken into the pan and baste with the sauce. Simmer for 5 minutes, or until the chicken is cooked through. Season to taste with salt and pepper and serve, sprinkled with coriander.

GOOD WITH Pilau rice or warm naan bread.

PREPARE AHEAD The dish can be made 1 day in advance, allowed to cool, covered, and chilled until needed. Reheat gently before serving.

serves 4

prep 20 mins,
plus marinating
• cook 25 mins

freeze for up to
3 months

Chicken with chorizo

In Mexico, chorizo is made with fresh pork, but in Spain, the pork is smoked first.

INGREDIENTS

3 tbsp olive oil
4 skinless chicken legs
250g (9oz) chorizo sausage,
   cut into bite-sized pieces
1 red onion, thinly sliced
1 tsp ground coriander
1 tsp chopped thyme
1 red pepper, skinned, deseeded,
   and chopped
1 yellow pepper, skinned, deseeded,
   and chopped
1 courgette, sliced
2 garlic cloves, crushed
400g can chopped tomatoes
200ml (7fl oz) chicken stock
60ml (2fl oz) dry sherry
freshly ground black pepper

METHOD

1 Preheat the oven to 180°C (350°F/Gas 4). Heat the oil in a large frying pan, add the chicken, and fry for 5–8 minutes, turning frequently, or until browned evenly. Transfer to a casserole dish.

2 Add the chorizo to the pan and fry for 2–3 minutes, or until lightly browned, stirring frequently. Remove and add to the casserole. Lower the heat, add the onion to the pan, and fry gently for 5 minutes, or until softened. Add the coriander, fry for 1 minute, then add the thyme, peppers, courgette, and garlic, and fry for 5 minutes.

3 Add the tomatoes, stock, and sherry. Season to taste with black pepper, and bring to the boil. Add the mixture into the casserole, cover, and cook in the oven for 40 minutes, or until the chicken is cooked through.

serves 4

prep 10 mins
• cook 1 hr
10 mins

freeze for up to
1 month

Coq au vin

A French classic that is perfect for entertaining – make the dish one day in advance and reheat when your guests arrive.

INGREDIENTS
2 tbsp plain flour
salt and freshly ground black pepper
1 large chicken, jointed
60g (2oz) butter
125g (4$\frac{1}{2}$oz) pancetta, cut into thick short strips
2 garlic cloves, crushed
1 carrot, cut into cubes
1 celery stick, roughly chopped
4 tbsp brandy or Cognac
750ml (1$\frac{1}{4}$ pints) red wine, such as Burgundy or Beaujolais
1 bay leaf
4–5 sprigs of thyme
1 tbsp olive oil
450g (1lb) button onions
1 tsp brown sugar
1 tsp red wine vinegar
225g (8oz) small mushrooms

METHOD

1 Season the flour with salt and pepper. Coat the chicken with 1 tbsp of the seasoned flour. Melt half the butter in the casserole, add the chicken, and fry gently until golden brown on all sides.

2 Add the pancetta, garlic, carrot, and celery, and fry until softened. Add the remaining flour and cook for 1–2 minutes. Pour in the brandy and wine, stirring to remove any sediment from the bottom of the casserole. Add the bay leaf and thyme, bring to the boil, cover, and simmer for 1 hour.

3 Meanwhile, melt the rest of the butter with the olive oil in a frying pan. Add the onions and fry until just brown. Stir in the sugar, vinegar, and 1 tbsp water.

4 Add the onions and mushrooms to the chicken, and cook for another 30 minutes, or until the chicken is cooked through and the vegetables are tender.

5 Transfer the chicken and vegetables to a hot serving dish. Discard the bay leaf and thyme. Skim off any excess fat and boil the sauce for 3–5 minutes, or until reduced. Pour over the chicken and serve.

GOOD WITH Mashed potatoes and French beans.

PREPARE AHEAD You can make this dish 1 day in advance. Cover and chill until needed.

serves 4

prep 30 mins
• cook 1 hr
30 mins

large flameproof
casserole

freeze for up to
3 months

SUPPER FOR FRIENDS

Duck confit

This French speciality from the Gascony region takes a little time to make, but is worth the wait.

INGREDIENTS

4 duck legs or 8 duck thighs
175g (6oz) coarse sea salt
30g (1oz) white peppercorns
1 tsp coriander seeds
5 juniper berries
4 garlic cloves, peeled and crushed
1 tbsp thyme leaves, chopped
1kg (2¼lb) duck fat or goose fat, melted

METHOD

1 Dry the duck legs or thighs on kitchen paper. Pound the sea salt with the peppercorns, coriander seeds, juniper berries, garlic, and thyme until all are roughly crushed into a paste. Rub the mixture into the duck skin, and put the duck, skin-side down, in a non-metallic dish. Cover with cling film and chill for 12 hours.

2 Preheat the oven to 140°C (275°F/Gas 1). Rinse the duck and pat dry, then put in a close-fitting ovenproof dish, and pour the melted fat over.

3 Cook for 1½ hours, or until cooked through and tender. It is cooked if a skewer slides in easily at the thickest part of the duck.

4 Transfer the confit to a plastic container. Ladle the fat over the duck through a fine sieve, being careful not to ladle in any of the juices from the bottom of the cooking dish. Cover the meat with at least 2.5cm (1in) of fat to keep the air from reaching it. Leave to cool in the fat, then transfer to the sealed Kilner jars or freezer bags, and refrigerate until needed.

5 When ready to serve, remove from the fat and pan-fry until heated through.

GOOD WITH Salad leaves and some roasted beetroot.

PREPARE AHEAD You can make this dish up to 4 weeks in advance. Keep in the refrigerator until needed. To give you plenty of time, start the confit at least 1 day before you plan to serve it.

serves 4

prep 15 mins, plus
chilling and curing
• cook 1½ hrs

4 medium
Kilner jars

freeze for up to
6 months

Baked poussin with lemon and paprika

A meltingly succulent dish that gets its subtle flavours from a blend of Egyptian and Spanish influences.

INGREDIENTS

4 lemons, plus extra, cut into wedges,
   to serve
4 large ripe tomatoes, peeled and chopped,
   or 225g can chopped tomatoes
1 large onion, finely chopped
1 tbsp paprika
sea salt
clear honey, or soft brown sugar
hot chilli powder
4 bay leaves, plus extra to garnish
4 poussins, cavity rinsed
8 garlic cloves
1–2 tsp balsamic vinegar
salt and freshly ground black pepper

METHOD

1 Preheat the oven to 200°C (400°F /Gas 6). Cut 2 of the lemons in half, then into thick slices. Put the tomatoes, onion, and lemon slices into the base of a casserole, sprinkle with the paprika, and mix together. Season with sea salt and add a drizzle of honey, or a sprinkling of brown sugar. Add the chilli powder to taste, then the bay leaves.

2 Cut the 2 remaining lemons into quarters. Insert 2 quarters into the cavity of each poussin, along with 2 cloves of the garlic. Lay poussins on top of the tomato mix in the casserole and season with sea salt.

3 Put the lid on the casserole and bake on the middle shelf for 20 minutes, then turn down the heat to 180°C (350°F/Gas 4) and cook, uncovered, for a further 25 minutes, or until cooked and browned. Remove the bird from the oven, place onto a serving plate, and keep warm.

4 Skim the fat from the juices in the pan and discard the lemon slices and bay leaves. Pour into a food processor or blender and process until smooth. Add the balsamic vinegar, then season to taste with salt and pepper. Serve the poussin with the sauce, garnished with bay leaves and lemon wedges.

serves 4

prep 15 mins
• cook 45 mins

low fat

freeze for up to
2 months

Creamy tarragon chicken

Fresh tarragon and cream is a classic pairing in French cuisine.

INGREDIENTS

30g (1oz) butter
1 tbsp rapeseed oil
4 chicken breasts, on the bone
250g (9oz) shallots, sliced
1 tsp dried *herbes de Provence*
2 garlic cloves, finely chopped
salt and freshly ground black pepper
250ml (8fl oz) hot chicken stock
120ml (4fl oz) dry white wine
250g (9oz) crème fraîche
2 tbsp chopped tarragon,
    plus extra sprigs to garnish

METHOD

1 Melt the butter with the oil in the casserole over medium-high heat. Add the chicken breasts, skin-side down, and fry for 3 minutes, or until golden brown, then turn over and continue browning for a further 2 minutes.

2 Keep the chicken breasts skin-side up, then sprinkle with the shallots, dried herbs, garlic, and salt and pepper to taste. Add the stock and wine and bring to the boil. Reduce the heat to low, cover the casserole and leave to simmer for 25 minutes, or until the chicken is tender and the juices run clear when pierced with a knife. Lift out the chicken and set aside, then boil the sauce until it is reduced by about half.

3 Stir in the crème fraîche and chopped tarragon, and continue cooking until thickened. If the sauce becomes too thick, add more chicken stock; adjust the seasoning, if necessary. Serve the chicken sliced off the bone, coated with the sauce and garnished with tarragon sprigs.

GOOD WITH Boiled long-grain rice, or try it with mashed potatoes with olive oil, black pepper, and chopped pitted black olives.

PREPARE AHEAD Steps 1 and 2 can be prepared up to 2 days in advance and kept in a covered container in the fridge. Reheat, making sure the chicken is completely heated through before stirring in the crème fraîche.

serves 4

prep 10 mins
• cook 35 mins

large flameproof
casserole

freeze the dish
after step 2,
once cooled
completely, for
up to 1 month;
thaw at room
temperature,
then complete
the recipe

Chicken with pancetta

Pancetta and chicken is always a winning combination. Add the olives and capers and you have a delicious dish, packed with Mediterranean flavours.

INGREDIENTS

2 tbsp flour
salt and freshly ground black pepper
6 chicken breasts, about 175g (6oz) each
4 tbsp olive oil
4 tbsp butter
4 garlic cloves, chopped
225g (8oz) pancetta, diced
2 tbsp white wine vinegar
4 tbsp capers
12 pitted black olives, chopped
2 tbsp chopped thyme
120ml (4fl oz) double cream

METHOD

1 Season the flour with salt and pepper. Toss the chicken in the seasoned flour and shake off the excess. Heat the oil and butter in a large frying pan and fry the garlic and pancetta over a medium-low heat for 3–4 minutes. Remove and set aside.

2 Add the chicken to the pan and brown on both sides. Return the pancetta and garlic to the pan and add the vinegar, capers, olives, and thyme. Lower the heat, cover, and cook for 35 minutes.

3 Remove the chicken; keep warm. Pour the cream into the pan and cook for 1–2 minutes to thicken. Serve the chicken with the sauce poured over.

serves 4

prep 15 mins
• cook 45 mins

Chicken in balsamic vinegar

This cold chicken dish has a lovely hint of sweetness from the balsamic vinegar and raisins.

INGREDIENTS

4 skinless boneless chicken breasts
salt and freshly ground black pepper
200ml (7fl oz) white wine
4 tbsp balsamic vinegar
200ml (7fl oz) fruity olive oil
2 tbsp fresh chopped basil or tarragon
zest of 1 lemon
4 tbsp raisins, soaked in boiling water
   for 10 mins and drained
rocket, to serve
watercress, to serve
1 lemon, cut into wedges, to serve
60g (2oz) pine nuts, toasted,
   to serve

METHOD

1 Preheat the oven to 190°C (375°F/Gas 5). Flatten the chicken breasts by placing them between two sheets of cling film and bashing gently with a rolling pin. Place the chicken in a lightly oiled, shallow roasting tin. Season with salt and pepper, then pour the wine over, cover with greaseproof paper and bake for 20 minutes, or until cooked through. Take the chicken out and set aside to cool in the tin. Reserve 2 tbsp of the cooking liquid.

2 Whisk together the balsamic vinegar and oil, then add the reserved cooking liquid. Add the basil, lemon zest, and raisins. Arrange the chicken in a dish, pour the dressing over, cover, and chill for 12 hours or overnight, turning the chicken once.

3 To serve, bring back to room temperature, slice thinly, and arrange on a serving plate. Pour the marinade over. Garnish with salad leaves and lemon wedges, then scatter with the pine nuts.

GOOD WITH Roasted cherry tomatoes on the vine, and hot, buttered new potatoes.

serves 6

**prep 50 mins,
plus marinating
• cook about
20 mins**

Garlic chicken

Based on a classic Indian dish called *Murg Massalam*, this recipe can be oven-cooked, grilled, or barbecued.

INGREDIENTS
1 medium-sized whole chicken,
   cut into 8 portions (see page 12),
   skin removed

For the marinade
1 tbsp clear honey or golden syrup
2 garlic cloves, peeled and crushed
1 tsp ground ginger
$\frac{1}{2}$ tsp cardamom seeds
$\frac{1}{2}$ tsp ground coriander
$\frac{1}{4}$ tsp ground cumin
$\frac{1}{4}$ tsp ground turmeric
2 tbsp fresh lemon juice
1 tsp salt
4 tbsp low-fat natural yogurt

METHOD
1 With a sharp knife, make a few slashes in the chicken flesh to ensure even cooking.

2 Make the marinade by mixing together all the ingredients in a large bowl. Place the chicken pieces into the marinade and mix until well coated. Cover and refrigerate for at least 1 hour to allow the flavours to develop.

3 Preheat the oven to 200°C (400°F/Gas 6) and line a deep roasting tin with foil. Arrange the chicken in the tin and pour in about 150ml (5fl oz) of cold water. Spoon any remaining marinade over the chicken pieces and bake for 30–40 minutes, or until the chicken pieces are golden and crisp on the outside and soft and tender inside.

4 Transfer to a heated serving dish and serve hot, or allow to cool completely if serving cold.

GOOD WITH Basmati rice, flavoured with a cinnamon stick and a few cardamom pods.

serves 4

prep 10 mins,
plus marinating
• cook 1 hr

freeze for up to
1 month

Duck breasts with mushroom sauce

Tender duck breasts are complemented by crisp white wine and tangy mushroom sauce.

INGREDIENTS

2 tbsp light olive oil
4 spring onions, chopped
175g (6oz) button mushrooms,
    halved or quartered
1 tbsp lemon juice
1 tbsp sun-dried tomato purée
1 tsp cornflour
300ml (10fl oz) chicken stock
2 tbsp chopped parsley,
    plus extra to garnish
salt and freshly ground black pepper
4 duck breasts
2–3 tbsp white wine

METHOD

1 Heat the oil in a frying pan and fry the spring onions and mushrooms over a low heat for 3 minutes, or until softened. Stir in the lemon juice and sun-dried tomato purée.

2 Mix the cornflour with a little of the stock until smooth. Bring the stock to the boil, then gradually stir in the cornflour mixture, until thickened and smooth. Add the chopped parsley and season to taste with salt and pepper. Set aside and keep warm.

3 Score the skin of the duck breasts a few times with a sharp knife. Heat the ridged grill pan over a medium-high heat, add the duck and grill for 10 minutes, or until cooked to your liking, turning once.

4 Remove the duck breasts from the pan and keep warm. Pour off the excess fat, then add the wine to the pan. Cook for 2 minutes, scraping the pan to incorporate any cooking juices or sediment, then pour into the reserved sauce.

5 Serve the duck immediately, with the sauce spooned over, and sprinkled with chopped parsley.

GOOD WITH Boiled new potatoes and asparagus.

serves 4

prep 20 mins
• cook 25 mins

ridged cast-iron
grill pan

Duck with shallot confit

The spices and melted honey lend comforting winter flavours to the duck.

INGREDIENTS
6 duck breasts
1 tbsp honey
$^1/_2$ tsp five-spice powder
salt and freshly ground black pepper

For the shallot confit
30g (1oz) fresh root ginger, peeled
   and crushed or finely grated
225g (8oz) shallots, sliced
150ml (5fl oz) clear honey
150ml (5fl oz) red wine vinegar

METHOD
1 To make the confit, place the ginger, shallots, and honey into a saucepan over a medium heat. Cook for 10 minutes, stirring often, or until the shallots are softened.

2 Stir in the vinegar and bring to the boil. Reduce the heat and simmer for 5–10 minutes, or until the confit is reduced and syrupy, stirring occasionally.

3 Add 150ml (5fl oz) water and cook for 5–10 minutes, or until the mixture is golden, and has thickened slightly.

4 Meanwhile, preheat the oven to 200°C (400°F/Gas 6). Trim any excess fat from the duck breasts and heat a heavy frying pan over a high heat. When the pan is hot, place the duck skin-side down and cook for 5 minutes, or until brown. Then turn and brown the other sides.

5 Place the duck breasts in a roasting tin and brush with honey. Add the five-spice powder, and season to taste with salt and pepper. Roast for 8–10 minutes, or until the middle is cooked through to your taste.

6 Remove from the oven and allow to rest for 5 minutes. Carve, and serve with the shallot confit.

GOOD WITH A sweet potato purée, sautéed pak choi, or mixed and dressed green beans.

PREPARE AHEAD The shallot confit can be made up to 3 days in advance, covered, and refrigerated until you're ready to serve.

serves 6

prep 10 mins
• cook 30 mins

Chicken biryani

For special occasions, this subtly spiced, aromatic dish from India is traditionally decorated with pieces of edible silver leaf.

INGREDIENTS
2 tbsp vegetable oil
30g (1oz) butter or ghee
1 large onion, thinly sliced
2 garlic cloves, crushed
6 curry leaves
6 cardamom pods
1 cinnamon stick, broken
   into 2 or 3 pieces
1 tsp ground turmeric
$1/2$ tsp ground cumin
4 skinless boneless chicken breasts,
   cut into 2.5cm (1in) pieces
3 tbsp mild curry paste
300g (10oz) basmati rice
85g (3oz) sultanas
900ml ($1^{1}/_{2}$ pints) chicken stock
2 tbsp flaked almonds, toasted

METHOD
1 Heat the oil and butter in a large deep saucepan, and gently fry the onion and garlic until softened and starting to turn golden. Add the curry leaves, cardamom pods, and cinnamon stick, and fry for 5 minutes, stirring occasionally.

2 Add the turmeric and cumin, fry for 1 minute, then add the chicken and stir in the curry paste.

3 Add the rice and sultanas, stir well, then pour in enough of the stock to cover the rice. Bring to the boil, lower the heat, and cook gently for 10–12 minutes, or until the rice is cooked, adding more stock if the mixture becomes dry.

4 Transfer to a serving dish, fluff up the rice with a fork, and serve with flaked almonds scattered over the top.

PREPARE AHEAD Although the biryani is best cooked and eaten straight away, it can be made ahead, placed in a shallow ovenproof dish, with a little extra melted butter or ghee poured on top, covered tightly, and baked until thoroughly heated.

serves 4

prep 20 mins
• cook 30 mins

low fat

Tandoori chicken

As tender and flavoursome as the classic restaurant dish, this recipe has a more natural colour.

INGREDIENTS

8 chicken pieces, such as breasts,
    thighs, and legs, skin removed
groundnut oil or sunflower oil, for greasing
60g (2oz) ghee or butter, melted
1 red onion, thinly sliced to serve
lemon wedges, to serve

For the tandoori marinade

1 onion, coarsely chopped
2 large garlic cloves
1cm ($^1\!/_2$in) piece fresh root ginger,
    peeled and coarsely chopped
3 tbsp fresh lemon juice
$^1\!/_4$ tsp salt
$1^1\!/_4$–$1^1\!/_2$ tsp chilli powder, to taste
1 tsp garam masala
pinch of turmeric
pinch of Kashmiri chilli powder
pinch of saffron powder

METHOD

1 Prick the chicken pieces with a fork, then place them in a non-metallic bowl and set aside.

2 To make the marinade, put the onion, garlic, and ginger in a blender or food processor and blend until a paste forms, scraping down the side of the bowl. Add the lemon juice, salt, and the spices, and process again.

3 Pour the marinade over the chicken and rub in well. Cover the bowl with cling film, and leave to marinate in the refrigerator for at least 3 hours, occasionally turning the chicken pieces.

4 Preheat the oven to 220°C (425°F/Gas 7) and remove the chicken from the fridge. Put a rack in a roasting pan lined with kitchen foil, shiny-side up, and grease the rack. Arrange the chicken on the rack, then brush with melted ghee. Roast for 20–25 minutes, or until the juices run clear.

5 Preheat the grill on its highest setting. Pour off the juices that have accumulated in the bottom of the pan. Brush the chicken with more ghee and place under the grill for 5–10 minutes, or until the edges are lightly charred. Serve with the onion slices and lemon wedges.

PREPARE AHEAD The chicken can be marinated for up to 24 hours in the refrigerator.

serves 4

prep 10–15
mins, plus at
least 3 hrs
marinating
• cook 25–35
mins

134

Chicken wrapped in pancetta and sage

This is a light but elegant main course to which you can add grilled peppers and olives.

INGREDIENTS

12 baby plum tomatoes, halved
3 tbsp olive oil, plus extra to drizzle
salt and freshly ground black pepper
3 large boneless skinless chicken breasts
12 sage leaves
12 slices of pancetta or Parma ham
baby salad leaves, watercress, or rocket

For the dressing

90ml (3fl oz) olive oil
2 tbsp cider vinegar
2 tsp chopped flat-leaf parsley
1 shallot, finely chopped
1 tsp brown sugar
salt and freshly ground black pepper

METHOD

1 Preheat the oven to 150°C (300°F/Gas 2). Put the tomatoes into a roasting tin, drizzle with olive oil, and season to taste with salt and pepper. Roast in the oven for 1 hour, or until slightly dried and caramelized.

2 To make the dressing, place the first 5 ingredients in a small bowl and whisk together until thickened slightly. Season to taste with salt and pepper.

3 Cut each chicken breast into 4 pieces. Top each with a sage leaf, then wrap as tightly as possible with a piece of pancetta.

4 Heat the olive oil in a large frying pan and brown the chicken pieces on each side. Lower the heat and continue to cook the chicken, turning, for 10 minutes, or until cooked through.

5 Serve the chicken with salad leaves and the roasted tomatoes, and drizzle over a little dressing.

PREPARE AHEAD The chicken can be wrapped 1 day in advance, covered with cling film, and chilled. The dressing can be made up to 1 week in advance and stored in an airtight container in a refrigerator.

serves 6

prep 20 mins
• cook 1 hr
15 mins

Poached guinea fowl with spiced lentils

This simple dish makes a healthy, satisfying winter main course.

INGREDIENTS
1.35kg (3lb) guinea fowl
2 carrots, cut into chunks
2 celery sticks, halved
2 shallots, halved
1 bay leaf
10 black peppercorns
2 tbsp olive oil
140g (5oz) pancetta, finely diced
1 garlic clove, crushed
1 small red chilli, deseeded
   and finely chopped
300g (10oz) dried Puy lentils,
   rinsed and well drained
4 tbsp chopped flat-leaf parsley
salt and freshly ground black pepper

METHOD
1 Put the guinea fowl in a pan with the carrots, celery, shallots, bay leaf, and peppercorns. Cover with cold water, bring to the boil, then simmer for 45 minutes, covered.

2 Lift the guinea fowl on to a plate; keep warm. Strain the poaching liquid back into the pan and boil for 10 minutes, or until reduced.

3 Meanwhile, heat the oil in a pan and fry the pancetta. Add the garlic and chilli, and fry gently for 2–3 minutes. Remove from the heat and add the lentils.

4 Pour 400ml (14fl oz) of the reduced stock into the lentils. Bring to the boil, then simmer, uncovered, for 15 minutes, stirring. Add more stock as necessary. Add the chopped parsley and season to taste with salt and pepper.

5 Meanwhile, remove the skin from the guinea fowl and cut into pieces.

6 Serve the lentils, topped with pieces of guinea fowl. Spoon over the stock, if desired.

serves 4

prep 20 mins
• cook 1 hr
15 mins

Lemon honey chicken with mustard mayonnaise

A simple but tasty dish that can be griddled, grilled, or barbecued.

INGREDIENTS

6 skinless boneless chicken breasts,
   about 175g (6oz) each
2 tbsp clear honey
2 garlic cloves, crushed
2 fresh red chillies, deseeded
   and finely chopped
juice of 1 lemon
3 tbsp light soy sauce
3 tbsp olive oil
4 tbsp balsamic vinegar
salt and freshly ground black pepper

For the mustard mayonnaise

2 egg yolks
$\frac{1}{2}$ tbsp mild mustard
2 tbsp sherry vinegar
200ml (7fl oz) sunflower oil
2 tbsp lemon juice
large bunch of basil

METHOD

1 Score a criss-cross pattern on one side of each chicken breast. Place in a shallow dish. Mix the honey, garlic, chilli, lemon juice, soy sauce, oil, and vinegar together, and season to taste with pepper. Pour the marinade over the chicken and turn the chicken to coat. Cover and chill for 2 hours.

2 To make the mayonnaise, place the egg yolks, mustard, and vinegar in a food processor, and season to taste with salt and pepper. With the motor running, slowly add the oil until it thickens. Continue to add the oil in a steady drizzle, then add lemon juice to taste and the basil. Chill for at least 1 hour.

3 Preheat the grill to high. Remove the chicken from the marinade and grill for 15–20 minutes, or until well coloured and cooked through, turning every 5 minutes, and basting well. Slice the chicken breasts and serve with the mayonnaise spooned over.

PREPARE AHEAD The mayonnaise can be made 1 day in advance and the chicken can marinate overnight.

serves 6

prep 25 mins,
plus marinating
• cook 15–20
mins

Chilli and orange duck

The traditional flavour combination of rich duck and tangy orange is given a modern twist in this recipe.

INGREDIENTS

6 small duck breasts, about 200g (7oz) each
sea salt and freshly ground black pepper
2 tbsp clear honey
drizzle of olive oil
2 spring onions, trimmed

For the sauce

3 large oranges
100g (3^1/$_2$oz) sugar
1 tbsp grated fresh root ginger
1 red chilli, deseeded and finely sliced
2 star anise
1 cinnamon stick
1 tbsp sweet chilli sauce
1 tbsp Thai fish sauce
1 tbsp rice vinegar
4 tbsp red wine

METHOD

1 Preheat the oven to 220°C (425°F/Gas 7). To make the sauce, peel the zest from 1 orange using a potato peeler and cut the zest into the strips. Juice the oranges to make 360ml (12fl oz) juice. Combine the orange zest and juice with the rest of the sauce ingredients in a saucepan and bring to the boil, stirring. Simmer, stirring occasionally, for 12 minutes, or until lightly syrupy.

2 Trim the duck breasts of excess fat. Season the breasts to taste with salt and pepper, and brush a little honey over the skin. Heat the oil in a frying pan, set over a medium-high heat, add the duck breasts, skin-side down, and fry for 3–4 minutes, or until crispy and golden. Turn over the breasts, then transfer them to the oven for 8–10 minutes, or until just cooked through and still pink in the middle. Rest for 5 minutes before serving.

3 Cut the spring onions into finger-length pieces, then slice into thin strips. Slice the duck breasts, arrange on warmed plates, and scatter with the shreds of spring onion. Spoon over the sauce.

GOOD WITH Sweet potato mash and crunchy steamed beans.

PREPARE AHEAD Make the sauce the day before and chill. Sear the duck up to 2 hours in advance and keep chilled. Cook in a preheated oven at 220°C (425°F/Gas 7) for 6–10 minutes when required.

serves 6

prep 15–20 mins
• cook 25–30 mins

Grilled poussins

Grilled poultry with herbs has a wonderful flavour and is perfect for
a light lunch.

INGREDIENTS

2 poussins, about 800g (1³/₄lb) each
2 tbsp butter, melted
1 tbsp lemon juice
1 tbsp Worcestershire sauce
¹/₂ tsp dried tarragon, crumbled
¹/₂ tsp dried thyme, crumbed
¹/₄ tsp salt

METHOD

1 Spatchcock each poussin. Cut down each side of the backbone and discard. Turn the bird
over, open out, and press down hard on the breastbone to flatten (see page 16). Preheat the
grill to high.

2 Place the melted butter in a bowl and stir in the lemon juice, Worcestershire sauce, herbs,
and salt. Place the poussins, skin-side down, on the grill pan rack. Brush the poussins with half
the butter mixture and grill 12cm (5in) from the heat source for 18–20 minutes, or until lightly
browned on one side and almost tender. Turn over, brush with the remaining butter mixture, and
grill for 10–15 minutes, or until they are cooked through and the juices run clear when pierced
with a sharp knife.

GOOD WITH Mediterranean roasted vegetables, such as aubergines and courgettes.

serves 4

prep 5 mins
• cook 30–35
mins

Duck breasts with cherries

Pan-fried duck with fresh cherries, when in season, is a treat for a smart dinner party.

INGREDIENTS
4 large duck breasts, about 350g (12oz) each
sea salt and freshly ground black pepper

For the sauce
15g ($^{1}/_{2}$oz) butter
1 shallot, finely chopped
1 tbsp maple syrup
1 sprig of rosemary
75ml (2$^{1}/_{2}$fl oz) ruby port
100ml (3$^{1}/_{2}$fl oz) chicken stock
400g (14oz) fresh dark red cherries, pitted

METHOD
1 Score the skin of each duck breast with a sharp knife and rub salt and pepper into the cuts.

2 Heat a heavy frying pan. Add the breasts, skin-side down, and fry over a medium-high heat for 3–4 minutes. Turn the breasts over and cook for a further 2 minutes. Reduce the heat and cook for 6–8 minutes, or until cooked through. Remove from the heat and rest for 5 minutes.

3 To make the sauce, melt the butter in a saucepan over a moderate heat and fry the shallot for 2–3 minutes, or until softened but not brown, stirring constantly.

4 Stir in the maple syrup, rosemary, and port, and bring to a boil. Simmer for 30 seconds, then add the stock and simmer, uncovered, for 3–4 minutes, or until slightly reduced. Add the cherries, and cook for a further 2 minutes to heat them. Season to taste with salt and pepper. Slice the duck and serve with cherry sauce spooned over.

PREPARE AHEAD Make the sauce up to 2 days in advance, and chill until you are ready to cook the duck.

serves 4

Prep 15 mins
• cook 20 mins

Crispy roast duck

Duck is a special-occasion dish in China, and this cooking method makes the most of its sweet, succulent flesh.

INGREDIENTS
1 duck, about 1.8kg (4lb)
1 tsp five-spice powder
3 tbsp oyster sauce
1 tsp salt

For the glaze
3 tbsp honey
1 tbsp dark soy sauce
2 tbsp rice wine or dry sherry

METHOD
1 Rinse the duck inside and out and pat dry with absorbent kitchen paper. Mix the five-spice powder, oyster sauce, and salt, and spread over and inside the bird.

2 Insert the meat hook through the neck end, or tie string around the neck to hang the duck. Place the duck in a colander in the sink, pour a kettle of boiling water over it, then pat dry with kitchen paper. Repeat this pouring and drying 5 times.

3 To make the glaze, put the honey, soy sauce, rice wine, and 150ml (5fl oz) water in a saucepan and bring to the boil. Reduce the heat, simmer for 10 minutes, or until sticky, then brush the glaze over the duck until thoroughly coated.

4 Hang the duck over a roasting tin or shallow tray in a well-ventilated place and leave for 4–5 hours, or until the skin is dry.

5 Preheat the oven to 230°C (450°F/Gas 8). Place the duck in a roasting tin, breast-side up, and pour 150ml (5fl oz) cold water into the tin. Roast for 20 minutes, reduce the oven to 180°C (350°F/Gas 4), and roast for 1 hour 15 minutes, or until the skin is crisp and golden.

6 Leave the duck to stand for 10 minutes, then joint and arrange the duck on a serving platter. Serve at once.

GOOD WITH Chinese pancakes, shredded spring onions, thin batons of cucumber, and hoisin sauce.

PREPARE AHEAD You can start preparing the duck the day before required, up to the end of step 4, as the recipe requires extra time.

serves 4

prep 1 hr 15 mins,
plus drying and
resting • cook
1 hr 35 mins

meat hook or
kitchen string

ROASTS

Chicken in a pot

A simple meal wonderfully flavoured with cider and root vegetables.

INGREDIENTS

2 tbsp sunflower oil
1 chicken, about 1.5kg (3lb 3oz),
    cleaned and trussed
1 tbsp plain flour
500ml (16fl oz) dry cider
250ml (8fl oz) chicken stock
1 bouquet garni
salt and freshly ground black pepper
350g (12oz) baby carrots, scraped
350g (12oz) baby new potatoes
2 leeks, thickly sliced
2 tbsp chopped parsley

METHOD

1 Preheat the oven to 160°C (325°F/Gas 3). Heat the oil in the casserole over a medium heat. Add the chicken and brown on all sides, then lift out and set aside. Sprinkle the flour into the casserole and cook, stirring, for 2 minutes. Stir in the cider and stock and bring to the boil.

2 Return the chicken to the casserole, breast-side up, and add the bouquet garni and salt and pepper to taste. Cover and put in the oven for 1¼ hours. Add the vegetables and baste the chicken.

3 Return the casserole to the oven for 30–45 minutes, or until the vegetables are tender and the chicken juices run clear when you pierce the thickest part of a leg.

4 Remove from the oven and leave the chicken to stand in the broth for 10 minutes, then taste and adjust the seasoning. Sprinkle with the parsley and serve hot.

PREPARE AHEAD Steps 1–3 can be prepared up to 2 days in advance. Slowly bring to the boil before completing step 4.

serves 4

prep 10 minutes
• cook 1¾ hrs

large flameproof
casserole

freeze after step 3, once cooled completely, for up to 3 months; thaw at room temperature, then reheat

Roast chicken

Impressive, classic, and simple to cook, the perfect roast chicken
is all about timing and turning.

INGREDIENTS

1 oven-ready chicken, about 2.2kg (5lb)
30g (1oz) butter or 2 tbsp olive oil
salt and freshly ground black pepper
300g (10oz) stuffing of your choice (optional)

METHOD

1 Preheat the oven to 200°C (400°F/Gas 6). Weigh the chicken and calculate the cooking time allowing 20 minutes per 450g (1lb), plus 20 minutes. Put the bird on a clean cutting board and remove the wishbone (see page 20).

2 Rub the bird with the butter, then season well with salt and pepper inside and out, and place in a roasting tin. (If you are stuffing your bird, it's worth taking the trouble to do so between the breast and the skin (see page 21). This will protect and flavour the breast as it cooks.)

3 Place the bird in the middle shelf of the oven and roast for the calculated time. Baste the chicken regularly and turn it breast-side down for about a third of the cooking time to ensure the meat cooks evenly.

4 To check whether the chicken is cooked, pierce the thickest part of the leg with a metal skewer or thin knife to see if the juices run clear. If the juices are still pink, cook for a further 15 minutes, then check again. Leave the bird to rest for 15 minutes, then carve and serve.

GOOD WITH Bread sauce, gravy, and a selection of steamed vegetables.

serves 6

prep 15 mins
• cook 20 mins
per 450g (1lb)
and an extra 20
mins, plus 15
minutes resting

low GI

French roast chicken

This traditional method of roasting uses frequent basting, producing a really succulent roast.

INGREDIENTS

4 tbsp chopped fresh herbs,
   such as tarragon and
   flat-leaf parsley
2 garlic cloves, finely chopped
115g (4oz) unsalted butter, softened
1 chicken, about 1.5kg (3lb 3oz)
1 lemon, pricked with a fork
120ml (4fl oz) dry white wine
500ml (16fl oz) chicken stock
salt and freshly ground black pepper

METHOD

1 Preheat the oven to 190°C (375°F/Gas 5). Add the herbs and garlic to the butter and combine. Ease your fingers between the breast skin and flesh of the chicken, being careful not to tear the skin, and spread the butter under the skin using your fingertips. Place the lemon inside the bird, then truss.

2 Put the chicken on a rack in a roasting pan. Pour all of the wine and three-quarters of the stock over the chicken, then season to taste with salt and pepper. Roast for 1 hour 25 minutes, or until the juices run clear when you pierce the thickest part of the leg. Using a large spoon, baste the bird with the pan juices during cooking. If the liquid evaporates from the bottom of the pan, add a little more wine.

3 Remove the chicken from the pan and allow to rest, covered with foil, for 10 minutes. Skim the fat from the pan, then add the remaining stock and bring to the boil, stirring, until slightly reduced, then strain into a jug and serve with the chicken.

PREPARE AHEAD The herb butter can be made up to 1 day in advance and kept chilled.

serves 4

prep 15 mins
• cook 1 hr
30 mins

Roast chicken with thyme and lemon

Lemon and thyme are traditional roasting ingredients and make a simple, yet delicious, glaze when added to the butter.

INGREDIENTS
1.8kg (4lb) chicken,
    jointed into 8 pieces
    (see page 12)
1 lemon
2 garlic cloves, peeled and crushed
15g (½oz) butter
1 tbsp olive oil
small bunch of thyme,
    leaves removed from stalks
salt and freshly ground black pepper
120ml (4fl oz) dry white wine

METHOD
1 Preheat the oven to 200°C (400°F/Gas 6). Place the chicken pieces in the roasting tin, in one layer.

2 Finely grate 2 tsp zest from the lemon, reserving the lemon. Place the zest in a bowl with the garlic, butter, oil, and thyme, and season to taste with salt and pepper. Beat with a wooden spoon to mix.

3 Dot the lemon and thyme butter evenly over the chicken pieces. Cut the reserved lemon into chunks and tuck around the chicken, then pour over the wine.

4 Roast the chicken, turning and basting the chicken pieces occasionally, for 50–60 minutes, or until the chicken is golden brown and cooked through and the juices run clear when the meat is pierced with a knife. Add a little more wine if the juices start to boil dry.

GOOD WITH A mixed salad and oven-baked potato wedges.

serves 4

prep 15 mins,
plus standing
• cook 1 hr

low fat

Roast guinea fowl with mustard sauce

Guinea fowl is less gamey in flavour than grouse.

INGREDIENTS

1 tbsp sunflower oil
4 guinea fowl breasts, skin removed
salt and freshly ground black pepper

For the mustard sauce

150ml (5fl oz) vermouth or sherry
150ml (5fl oz) chicken stock
200ml (7fl oz) double cream
2 tsp wholegrain mustard
4–5 sprigs of chives, snipped

METHOD

1 Preheat the oven to 240°C (475°F/Gas 9). Heat the oil in a frying pan and brown the guinea fowl. Transfer to a roasting tin and season to taste with salt and pepper. Roast for 8–10 minutes, or until the juices run clear when pierced with a knife. Cover and leave to rest for 5 minutes.

2 To make the sauce, bring the vermouth to the boil in a pan, then simmer until reduced by half. Add the stock, return to the boil, then simmer to reduce again. Add the cream and simmer until thick enough to coat the back of a spoon.

3 Whisk the mustard and chives into the sauce. Season to taste with salt and pepper. Carve the guinea fowl to serve and spoon over the mustard sauce.

GOOD WITH Buttered new potatoes and sautéed onions.

serves 4

prep 40 mins
• cook 25 mins

Roast goose

Goose meat is rich in flavour, making it a perfect choice for a festive dinner party or special Sunday meal.

INGREDIENTS

1 large oven-ready goose,
  about 5kg (11¼lb)
salt and freshly ground black pepper
2 small onions, halved
1 tbsp olive oil
150ml (5fl oz) red wine
sprigs of sage, to garnish

METHOD

1 Preheat the oven to 180°C (350°F/Gas 4). Weigh the goose and calculate the cooking time, allowing 30 minutes per 1kg (2¼lb), plus 20 minutes. Prick the skin all over with a fork, rub with salt, and sprinkle with pepper. Tuck half the onion in the neck cavity and the other half into the body cavity. Brush with the olive oil.

2 Place the goose, breast-side up, on a rack in a roasting tin, and roast for the calculated time.

3 About 40 minutes before the goose is finished cooking, remove from the oven and lift off the foil. Carefully pour out the excess fat from the tin and set aside. Brush the leftover juices evenly over the skin. Return to the oven and repeat the brushing every 15 minutes until the goose is a rich amber-brown colour.

4 To test whether the goose is cooked, pierce the thickest part of a leg with a metal skewer or thin knife to see if the juices run clear. If the juices are still pink, cook for a further 15 minutes, then check again.

5 Remove the goose, cover with foil, and leave to stand for 15–20 minutes before carving (see pp22–23). Skim the excess fat from the juices and pour in the wine over a medium heat, stirring to loosen the sediment. Boil to reduce slightly, then add the remaining glaze, and serve alongside the goose. Garnish with the sage leaves to serve.

GOOD WITH A selection of roast vegetables, such as potatoes, carrots, and parsnips.

serves 4

prep 20 mins
• cook 3 hrs

freeze, cooked,
for up to
3 months

Roast turkey with cranberry pistachio stuffing

The light stuffing is great cooked inside the turkey, but can also be cooked separately.

INGREDIENTS

4.5kg (10lb) oven-ready turkey
15g ($^1/_2$oz) butter
8 streaky bacon rashers
fresh herbs, to garnish (optional)

For the stuffing

45g (1$^1/_2$oz) butter
1 onion, finely chopped

125g (4$^1/_2$oz) fresh white breadcrumbs
2 tbsp finely chopped parsley
115g (4oz) fresh or frozen cranberries,
  roughly chopped
60g (2oz) pistachio nuts, chopped
salt and freshly ground black pepper
2 egg whites
1–2 tbsp milk, to mix

METHOD

1 To make the stuffing, melt the butter in a frying pan, add the onion, and fry over a medium heat, stirring occasionally, for 3–4 minutes, or until softened.

2 Remove from the heat and stir in the breadcrumbs, parsley, cranberries, and pistachios. Season to taste with salt and pepper. Leave to cool. Stir in the egg whites with a little milk to make a firm mixture.

3 Preheat the oven to 180°C (350°F/Gas 4). Stuff the neck end of the turkey with enough stuffing to fill the cavity, reserving the rest. Weigh the stuffed turkey and calculate the cooking time of the turkey, allowing 20 minutes per 450g (1lb) plus 20 minutes extra.

4 Brush the melted butter over the turkey skin. Sprinkle with salt and pepper, place in a roasting tin, and cover loosely with foil. Roast the turkey for the calculated time, or until there is no trace of pink in the juices when pierced through the thickest part. Baste occasionally and remove the foil for the last 30–40 minutes of cooking to brown the bird.

5 Roll the remaining stuffing into 8 walnut-sized balls. Stretch the bacon rashers out thinly with the back of a knife, then cut in half crossways. Roll a piece of bacon around each stuffing ball and place on a lightly oiled baking sheet.

6 When the turkey is cooked, remove from the oven, cover with foil and leave to rest for at least 20 minutes before carving. Increase the oven temperature to 200°C (400°F/Gas 6), place the stuffing balls in the oven and cook for 15–20 minutes, or until golden brown. Serve the turkey with the stuffing balls and garnish with herbs, if desired.

GOOD WITH All the traditional accompaniments, such as roast potatoes, Brussels sprouts, carrots, and gravy.

serves 6-8

prep 30 mins
• cook 3 hrs
45 mins

low fat

freeze the
cooked turkey
and stuffing for
up to 3 months

LEFTOVERS

Chicken stock

For a clear stock, make sure you remove any fat from the chicken before boiling, or it will turn cloudy. For a dark, golden stock, leave the onion unpeeled.

INGREDIENTS

1 chicken carcass,
   skin and fat removed
2 celery sticks, roughly chopped
1 onion, quartered
few sprigs of flat-leaf parsley
few sprigs of thyme
1 bay leaf
$^{1}/_{2}$ tsp salt
5 black peppercorns, lightly crushed

METHOD

1 Put the chicken pieces, celery, onion, herbs, and salt in a large pan with 2 litres (3$^{1}/_{2}$ pints) cold water and bring to boiling point over a high heat. Using a slotted spoon, skim off any foam as it rises to the surface. Reduce the heat to low, then add the peppercorns, partially cover the pan, and leave to simmer for about 1 hour.

2 Strain the stock into a large bowl, discarding the flavourings. It is now ready to use.

PREPARE AHEAD You can make the stock up to 2 days in advance. Leave to cool completely, then store in the refrigerator; lift off any fat that has risen to the surface. Bring to the boil before using.

**makes 1 litre
(1¾ pints)**

**prep 10 mins
• cook 1 hr**

**freeze for up to
6 months**

Club sandwich

This hearty sandwich of cooked chicken, bacon, tomatoes, and lettuce is layered between slices of toasted bread and is guaranteed to satisfy those hunger pangs.

INGREDIENTS

1 small garlic clove, crushed
1 tsp dried mixed herbs
2 tbsp olive oil
salt and freshly ground black pepper
3 boneless chicken breasts
16 streaky bacon rashers
12 slices of white bread
4 tbsp mayonnaise
1 tsp wholegrain mustard
butter, for spreading
4 ripe tomatoes, sliced
2 Little Gem lettuces, shredded
8 cornichons

METHOD

1 In a bowl mix together the garlic, herbs, and 1 tbsp of the olive oil. Season to taste with salt and pepper. Toss the chicken breasts in the mixture and set aside for at least 30 minutes.

2 Meanwhile, heat a large frying pan and pour in the remaining olive oil. Fry the bacon in batches for 2–3 minutes, or until crisp and golden. Drain on kitchen paper.

3 Using the same frying pan, add the chicken breasts, skin-side down, and cook for 4–5 minutes, or until the skin is nicely golden. Then turn over and cook for a further 4–5 minutes, or until cooked. Set aside on a plate to rest.

4 Meanwhile, toast the slices of bread and lay them out on a large chopping board, ready to start assembling the sandwich. Remove the crusts, if desired.

5 In a bowl, mix together the mayonnaise and mustard, and season to taste with salt and pepper.

6 Spread the toast with the butter and the mustard mayonnaise. Slice the chicken breasts and arrange half of the pieces on 4 of the toast slices. Cut the bacon strips in half and evenly lay half on top of the chicken. Top with tomato slices followed by shredded lettuce. Top with a piece of toast and repeat the filling layer. Finish off by placing the remaining slices of toast on top.

7 Cut each sandwich in half, diagonally. Top with a cornichon and push a cocktail stick down through the centre of each sandwich to hold it altogether.

GOOD WITH Gherkins and other pickles on the side.

PREPARE AHEAD Steps 1 and 5 can be made several hours in advance.

serves 4

prep 15 mins,
plus marinating
• cook 15 mins

Meaty spring rolls

"Spring" rolls are so named because they were eaten to celebrate the Chinese New Year, or first day of spring.

INGREDIENTS
225g (8oz) cooked ham, chopped,
  or other meats such as pork or beef
½ red pepper, deseeded and finely chopped
115g (4oz) mushrooms, chopped
4 spring onions, thinly sliced
115g (4oz) beansprouts
2cm (¾in) fresh root ginger, grated
1 tbsp rice wine vinegar
1 tbsp soy sauce
vegetable oil, for shallow frying
225g (8oz) cooked chicken, chopped
1 tbsp cornflour
12 spring roll wrappers
6 Chinese cabbage leaves, halved
sweet chilli dipping sauce, to serve

METHOD

1 In a bowl, mix together the ham, red pepper, mushrooms, spring onions, beansprouts, ginger, vinegar, and soy sauce.

2 Heat 2 tbsp oil in a frying pan, add the ham mixture, and stir-fry for 3 minutes. Set aside to cool, then stir in the chicken.

3 In a small bowl, mix the cornflour with 4 tbsp cold water.

4 Lay a wrapper on a work surface and top with half a cabbage leaf and 1 tbsp of the ham mixture. Brush the edges of the wrapper with the cornflour mix and roll up, tucking in the sides and pressing the brushed edges together to seal. Repeat with the remaining wrappers and filling.

5 Shallow-fry the rolls in hot oil until golden brown on all sides. Drain on kitchen paper and serve at once with sweet chilli dipping sauce.

PREPARE AHEAD Make the filling up to 3 hours in advance and fill the rolls just before frying.

makes 12

prep 25 mins
• cook 15 mins

172

Calzone

These crescent-shaped folded pizzas can be filled with almost any pizza topping, but this is the most popular.

INGREDIENTS

500g (1lb 2oz) strong white flour,
  plus extra for dusting
2 x 7g sachets fast-action dried yeast
½ tsp salt
2 tbsp olive oil

For the filling
3 tbsp olive oil
6 back bacon rashers, chopped

1 skinless boneless chicken breast,
  cut into small pieces
1 green pepper, deseeded and chopped
4 tbsp sun-dried tomato paste
200g (7oz) mozzarella cheese, sliced
4 tbsp chopped flat-leaf parsley
freshly ground black pepper
beaten egg, to seal

METHOD

1 Put the flour in a mixing bowl, stir in the yeast and salt. Add the olive oil and 350ml (12fl oz) tepid water, then mix to a dough. Knead on a floured surface for 10 minutes, or until smooth.

2 Roll the dough into a ball, and place in a lightly oiled bowl. Cover loosely with the oiled cling film. Leave in a warmed place until the dough has doubled in size.

3 Preheat the oven to 200°C (400°F/Gas 6). Transfer the dough to a lightly floured surface, knead lightly, divide into 4, and roll out to 23cm (9in) rounds. Lift on to greased baking sheets.

4 Heat 1 tbsp of the oil in a frying pan and fry the bacon, chicken, and green pepper for 5 minutes, or until the bacon and chicken are lightly browned, stirring frequently. Remove from the pan and set aside to cool.

5 Spread the tomato paste over half of each dough round, keeping well within the edges. Top with bacon, chicken, green pepper, mozzarella, and parsley and season with plenty of black pepper.

6 Brush the edges of the dough with beaten egg and fold over the plain half of each round to enclose the filling, pressing the edges together firmly with your fingers or a fork to seal.

7 Brush with the remaining olive oil and bake for 20–25 minutes, or until puffed, crisp, and golden brown. Serve hot.

GOOD WITH A green salad.

PREPARE AHEAD The dough can be prepared the day before and stored in the refrigerator. The low temperature will retard the yeast, but if the dough rises to double its size, lightly knead and use as required.

serves 4

**prep 35 mins,
plus rising
and cooling
• cook 45–55
mins**

Cock-a-leekie soup

The traditional method involves the slow simmering of a whole chicken, but today it can be prepared with less time and effort.

INGREDIENTS
450g (1lb) chicken breasts
   and thighs, skinned
2 bay leaves
1 litre (1³/₄ pints) chicken stock
   or vegetable stock
60g (2oz) long-grain rice
2 leeks, thinly sliced
2 carrots, grated
pinch of ground cloves
1 tsp sea salt
1 tbsp chopped parsley

METHOD
1 Place the chicken in a pan with the bay leaves and pour in the stock. Bring to the boil then reduce the heat, cover, and simmer for 30 minutes.

2 Skim the surface of the soup and discard any scum that has formed. Add the rice, vegetables, cloves, and salt, bring back to the boil, reduce the heat, cover, and simmer for a further 30 minutes.

3 Remove the bay leaves and discard. If you wish, you can lift out the chicken, remove the meat from the bones, then return the meat to the soup.

4 Ladle the soup into a warm tureen or divide between individual serving bowls and serve while still hot, sprinkled with the chopped parsley.

GOOD WITH Plenty of warm crusty bread. To make an even more substantial meal, add a few boiled potatoes to each serving.

serves 4

prep 10 mins
• cook 1½ hrs

low fat

freeze for up to
3 months

Chicken noodle soup

This spicy Mexican soup, *Sopa Seca de Fideos*, is made with thin fideo noodles, which are similar to angel hair pasta.

INGREDIENTS

2 large ripe tomatoes,
   skinned and deseeded
2 garlic cloves
1 small onion, roughly chopped
2 dried chipotle chillies, soaked
900ml (1½ pints) chicken stock
3 tbsp vegetable oil
2 skinless boneless chicken breasts, diced
225g (8oz) Mexican fideo
   or dried angel hair pasta
4 tbsp soured cream, to serve
1 avocado, stone removed
   and chopped, to serve

METHOD

1 Put the tomatoes, garlic, onion, chillies, and 2 tbsp stock into a food processor or blender, and process to a purée. Set aside.

2 Heat 2 tbsp oil in a large pan and stir-fry the chicken for 2–3 minutes, or until just cooked. Remove from the pan, drain on kitchen paper, and set aside.

3 Add the remaining oil to the pan, add the noodles, and cook over a low heat until the noodles are golden, stirring constantly.

4 Pour in the tomato mixture, stir until the noodles are coated, then add the stock, and return the chicken to the pan. Cook the noodles for 2–3 minutes, or until just tender.

5 To serve, ladle into soup bowls, and top each with soured cream and chopped avocado.

PREPARE AHEAD The tomato sauce base for the soup can be prepared 1 day in advance. Chill until needed.

serves 4

prep 20 mins
• cook 15 mins

soak the dried
chillies in water
for 30 mins

low fat

Warm chicken salad

Quick to cook and easy to assemble, this is an example of a French *salade tiède,* or warm salad.

INGREDIENTS

4 tbsp extra virgin olive oil
4 chicken breasts, about 150g
  (5^1/$_2$oz) each, cut into thin strips
1 garlic clove, finely chopped
60g (2oz) sun-dried tomatoes, thinly sliced
salt and freshly ground black pepper
1 small head of radicchio, torn into small pieces
250g (9oz) asparagus spears,
  each trimmed and cut into 3 pieces
2 tbsp raspberry vinegar
^{1}/$_2$ tsp sugar

METHOD

1 Heat 2 tbsp of the oil in a large non-stick frying pan over a medium-high heat. Add the chicken and garlic and fry, stirring, for 5–7 minutes, or until the chicken is tender and cooked through. Stir in the sun-dried tomatoes, and season to taste with salt and pepper.

2 Meanwhile, put the radicchio leaves in a large serving bowl. Remove the chicken from the pan, using a slotted spoon, and place in the bowl with the radicchio.

3 Add the asparagus to the fat remaining in the pan and fry, stirring constantly, for 1–2 minutes, or until just tender. Transfer to the bowl with the chicken.

4 Whisk together the remaining 2 tbsp oil, the vinegar, and sugar, then pour into the pan and stir over a high heat until well combined. Pour this dressing over the salad and toss quickly so that all the ingredients are well mixed and coated with the dressing. Serve straight away.

serves 4

prep 10 mins
• cook 8 mins

Chicken and noodle stir-fry

A colourful Chinese favourite, packed with contrasting flavours and textures.

INGREDIENTS

vegetable oil, for frying
2 skinless boneless chicken breasts,
    cut into bite-sized pieces
$1/2$ red pepper, deseeded and chopped
$1/2$ green pepper, deseeded and chopped
$1/2$ yellow pepper or orange pepper,
    deseeded and chopped
2.5cm (1in) piece of fresh root ginger,
    peeled and grated
115g (4oz) shiitake mushrooms, quartered
120ml (4fl oz) chicken stock
2 tbsp tomato ketchup
2 tbsp light soy sauce
1 tsp cornflour
350g (12oz) fresh medium egg noodles
few drops of toasted sesame oil
2 tbsp sesame seeds, for garnish

METHOD

1 Heat 1 tbsp of the vegetable oil in the wok until hot. Add the chicken and stir-fry for 3 minutes. Remove and set aside.

2 Add the peppers, ginger, and mushrooms to the wok and stir-fry for 3 minutes.

3 Mix together the chicken stock, ketchup, soy sauce, and cornflour until smooth. Return the chicken to the wok, add the noodles, and pour in the stock mixture. Toss everything together over the heat for 3 minutes, or until piping hot.

4 Just before serving, drizzle with sesame oil, sprinkle the sesame seeds on top, and serve.

serves 4

prep 20 mins
• cook 10 mins

wok

Chicken croquettes

These golden, savoury nuggets, crunchy outside and meltingly soft inside, are a popular Spanish first course.

INGREDIENTS

100g (3^1/$_2$oz) butter
115g (4oz) flour
750ml (1^1/$_4$ pints) milk
400g (14oz) cooked chicken, shredded
2 tsp tomato purée
salt and freshly ground black pepper
8–9 tbsp fine breadcrumbs
3 eggs, beaten
oil, for shallow frying

METHOD

1 Melt the butter in a saucepan over a medium-low heat and add the flour, stirring continuously. Cook the mixture for 1–2 minutes, then stir in the milk to make a smooth, thick sauce.

2 Add the shredded chicken and the tomato purée and season to taste with salt and pepper. Continue to cook for 5 minutes, or until the mixture thickens. Remove the pan from the heat and leave to cool completely.

3 Use two spoons to form croquettes about 3–4cm (1^1/$_2$–2in) long. Roll them in the breadcrumbs, coat in the egg, and roll in the breadcrumbs again.

4 Heat the oil in a heavy frying pan. When hot, fry the croquettes in batches for 5 minutes, turning frequently, until they are golden all over. Remove with a slotted spoon and drain on kitchen paper.

5 Transfer the croquettes to a heated serving plate and serve while still hot.

GOOD WITH Garlic mayonnaise or *Salsa Rosa*, made from 2 parts mayonnaise to 1 part tomato ketchup. The croquettes can also be served cold, making them excellent picnic food.

PREPARE AHEAD The béchamel sauce can be prepared ahead and allowed to cool. The croquettes can be made up to 24 hours in advance and fried before serving.

serves 4

prep 30 mins
• cook 20 mins

freeze for up to
3 months

Chicken chow mein

This popular one-pot Chinese dish is a colourful, tasty medley of noodles, chicken, mushrooms, and vegetables.

INGREDIENTS

4 tsp vegetable oil
4 spring onions,
    cut into 2.5cm (1in) lengths
2cm (³/₄in) piece of fresh root ginger,
    peeled and grated
140g (5oz) shiitake mushrooms
    or oyster mushrooms, sliced
1 red pepper, deseeded and chopped
6 skinless boneless chicken thighs,
    cut into bite-sized pieces
115g (4oz) green beans,
    cut into 2.5cm (1in) lengths
350g (12oz) fresh fine egg noodles
4 tbsp light soy sauce,
    plus extra for sprinkling
1 tbsp rice wine or dry sherry
120ml (4fl oz) chicken stock
1 tsp cornflour

METHOD

1 Heat half the oil in a wok or large frying pan and stir-fry the spring onions, ginger, mushrooms, and red pepper over high heat for 5 minutes. Remove and set aside.

2 Add the remaining oil and stir-fry the chicken over a high heat for 3 minutes, in separate batches if necessary, then remove from the pan and set aside.

3 Add the green beans and stir-fry for 2 minutes. Add the noodles and return the chicken and vegetables to the pan.

4 Mix together the soy sauce, wine, stock, and cornflour until smooth and well blended, then pour into the pan. Toss everything together for 2 minutes, or until piping hot.

5 Serve immediately, with extra soy sauce to sprinkle over.

GOOD WITH Other Chinese dishes, as part of a themed meal.

PREPARE AHEAD The vegetables and chicken can be chopped several hours in advance and kept in covered bowls in the refrigerator.

serves 4

prep 15 mins
• cook 15 mins

low fat

Chicken pasties

A complete and filling lunch in a pastry packet.

INGREDIENTS
For the pastry
350g (12oz) plain flour
175g (6oz) butter, chilled and diced
2 eggs

For the filling
115g (4oz) cream cheese
6 spring onions, sliced
2 tbsp chopped flat-leaf parsley
salt and freshly ground black pepper
2–3 chicken breasts, about 350g (12oz),
   cut into 2cm ($^3/_4$in) chunks
1 potato, about 150g (5$^1/_2$oz),
   cut into 1cm ($^1/_2$in) cubes
1 sweet potato, about 150g (5$^1/_2$oz),
   cut into 1cm ($^1/_2$in) cubes

METHOD
1 To make the pastry, sift the flour into a bowl, then rub in the butter until the mixture resembles fine breadcrumbs. Beat the eggs and 3 tbsp of cold water together. Set aside 1 tbsp of the mixture for glazing, and pour the rest over the dry ingredients, and mix to a dough. Wrap in oiled cling film and chill for 20 minutes.

2 Meanwhile, mix the cream cheese, onions, and parsley in a bowl, and season to taste with salt and pepper. Stir in the chicken, potato, and sweet potato.

3 Preheat the oven to 200°C (400°F/Gas 6). Divide the pastry into 4 pieces. Roll out each piece on a lightly floured surface and, using a small plate as a guide, cut into a 20cm (8in) round.

4 Spoon a quarter of the filling into the centre of each round. Brush the edges with water and bring together to seal, then crimp.

5 Place the pasties on a baking sheet and brush with the reserved egg mixture. Make a slit in the tops and bake for 10 minutes, then reduce the heat to 180°C (350°F/Gas 4) and cook for 25–30 minutes, or until a thin knife comes out clean when inserted into the centre.

6 Remove from the oven and serve the pasties hot or cold.

serves 4

prep 30 mins,
plus chilling
• cook 35 mins

Chicken jalousie

Although it looks impressive, this dish is quick to make with shop-bought puff pastry and cooked chicken.

INGREDIENTS

25g (scant 1oz) butter
2 leeks, thinly sliced
1 tsp chopped fresh thyme
   or $1/2$ tsp dried thyme
1 tsp plain flour, plus extra for dusting
90ml (3fl oz) chicken stock
1 tsp lemon juice
500g packet puff pastry
300g (10oz) skinless boneless
   cooked chicken, chopped
salt and freshly ground black pepper
1 egg, beaten, to glaze

METHOD

1 Melt the butter in a saucepan. Add the leeks and cook over a low heat, stirring frequently, for 5 minutes, or until fairly soft. Stir in the thyme, then sprinkle over the flour and stir in. Gradually blend in the stock and bring to the boil, stirring until thickened. Remove from the heat, stir in the lemon juice, and leave to cool.

2 Meanwhile, preheat the oven to 220°C (425°F/Gas 7). Roll out just under half of the pastry on a lightly floured work surface to a 25 x 15cm (10 x 6in) rectangle. Lay the pastry on a large dampened baking sheet. Roll out the remaining pastry to a 25 x 18cm (10 x 7in) rectangle, lightly dust with flour, then fold in half lengthways. Make cuts 1cm ($1/2$in) apart along the folded edge to within 2.5cm (1in) of the outer edge.

3 Stir the chopped chicken into the leek mixture and season generously with salt and pepper. Spoon evenly over the pastry base, leaving a 2.5cm (1in) border. Dampen the edges of the pastry with water. Place the second piece of pastry on top and press the edges together to seal; trim off the excess. Brush the top with beaten egg and bake for 25 minutes, or until golden brown and crisp. Leave to cool for a few minutes before serving.

GOOD WITH Roasted vegetables, such as shallots, courgettes, peppers, and aubergines.

serves 4

prep 25 mins
• cook 25 mins

Rice porridge

Known in Asia as Rice Congee or *Jook*, this dish is eaten for breakfast in China when the weather is cold.

INGREDIENTS

6 dried Chinese mushrooms
2 tbsp vegetable oil
1cm ($\frac{1}{2}$in) piece fresh root ginger,
　peeled and grated
1 garlic clove, finely chopped
1 carrot, cut julienne
$\frac{1}{2}$ tsp dried chilli flakes
200g (7oz) long-grain rice
900ml ($1\frac{1}{2}$ pints) chicken stock
2 skinless boneless chicken breasts,
　cut into small pieces
4 spring onions, chopped
2 tbsp light soy sauce
freshly ground black pepper
2 tbsp chopped coriander

METHOD

1 Put the mushrooms in a bowl and pour over enough boiling water to cover. Set aside for 20 minutes to soak. Drain, reserving the soaking water, then snip the mushrooms into small pieces using kitchen scissors.

2 Heat the oil in a wok or large frying pan, add the ginger, garlic, carrot, and chilli, and fry gently for 5 minutes. Stir in the rice and add the stock. Measure 150ml (5fl oz) of the soaking water from the mushrooms and strain this into the pan.

3 Bring to a simmer and cook for 20 minutes, then add the chicken and cook for a further 30 minutes, or until the rice has broken down to a porridge-like consistency. Stir in the spring onions and soy sauce. Season to taste with black pepper. Serve hot, sprinkled with chopped coriander.

PREPARE AHEAD Although best fresh, the porridge can be prepared in advance and reheated, adding stock or water if it has become too thick.

serves 4

prep 20 mins,
plus standing
• cook 1 hr

low fat

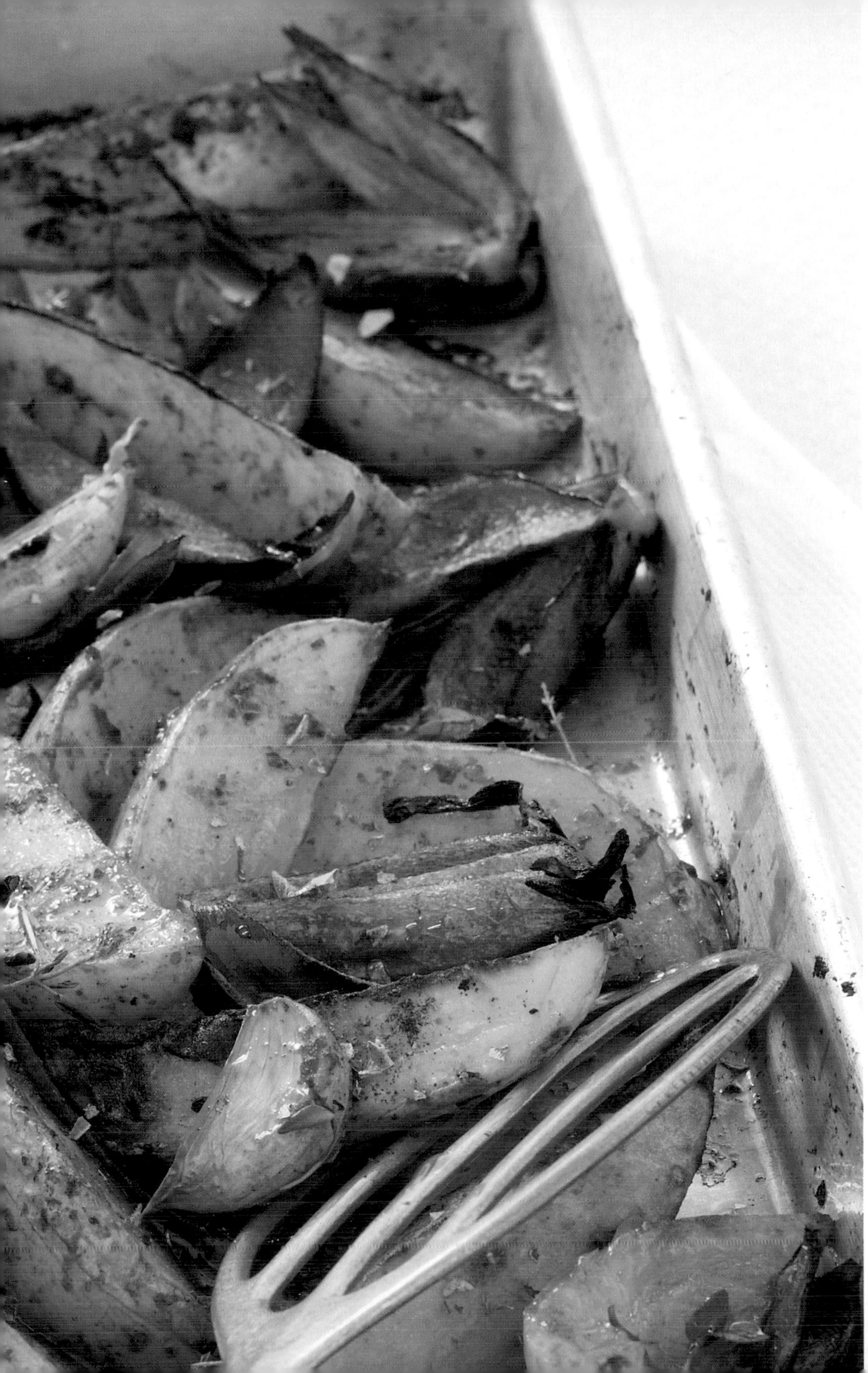

ACCOMPANIMENTS

Rice and peas

In this West Indian dish, the "peas" are known as gungo peas in Jamaica and pigeon peas in Trinidad.

INGREDIENTS

400g can gungo peas or black-eyed peas,
  drained and rinsed
400ml can coconut milk
1 large onion, finely chopped
1 green pepper, deseeded and chopped
salt and freshly ground black pepper
125g (4$^{1}/_{2}$oz) long-grain rice
chilli powder, to garnish

METHOD

1 Put the peas, coconut milk, onion, and green pepper in a saucepan. Season to taste with salt and pepper and simmer over a low heat for 5 minutes.

2 Stir in the rice, cover, and cook gently for 35 minutes, or until the rice is tender, stirring. Serve sprinkled with chilli powder.

PREPARE AHEAD The dish can be prepared in advance and reheated until piping hot at 180°C (350°F/Gas 4) in a shallow dish tightly covered with foil.

serves 4

prep 10 mins
• cook 45 mins

Cajun-spiced potato wedges

This peppery dish was developed by the French settlers of Louisiana.

INGREDIENTS

4 potatoes, unpeeled
1 lemon, cut into 6 wedges
12 garlic cloves
3 red onions, cut into 8 wedges
4 bay leaves
3 tbsp lemon juice
1 tbsp tomato purée
salt and freshly ground black pepper
1 tsp paprika
$1/2$ tsp cayenne pepper
1 tsp dried oregano
1 tsp dried thyme
$1/2$ tsp ground cumin
6 tbsp olive oil

METHOD

1 Preheat the oven to 200°C (400°F/Gas 6). Cut the potatoes into thick wedges. Cook in a large pan of salted boiling water for 3 minutes, then drain well and place in a large roasting tin with the lemon, garlic, onions, and bay leaves.

2 Whisk together the remaining ingredients with 6 tbsp water and pour evenly over the potatoes; toss well to coat.

3 Roast for 30–40 minutes, or until the potatoes are tender and the liquid has been absorbed. Gently turn the potatoes frequently during cooking using a fish slice. Serve hot.

PREPARE AHEAD The potatoes can be prepared, up to the end of step 2, several hours in advance.

serves 6

prep 10 mins
• cook 35–45 mins

Roast sweet potato with sesame glaze

Roasting sweet potato brings out its natural sweetness.

INGREDIENTS

5 sweet potatoes, peeled
2 tbsp olive oil
sea salt and freshly ground black pepper
1 tbsp clear honey
1 tbsp light soy sauce
2 tbsp sesame seeds

METHOD

1 Preheat oven to 200°C (400°F/Gas 6). Cut the potatoes into large chunks and place on a roasting tin, drizzle with olive oil, and season with salt and pepper. Roast the potatoes for 30 minutes, turning halfway through, or until just tender.

2 Mix together the honey, soy sauce, and sesame seeds, then add the potato chunks, toss until coated, and roast for a further 20 minutes, or until well coloured.

serves 6

prep 10 mins
• cook 50 mins

Polenta

This cornmeal "porridge" is served in northern Italy as an accompaniment to meat dishes.

INGREDIENTS

1.4 litres (2$\frac{1}{2}$ pints) chicken stock
  or vegetable stock
350g (12oz) quick-cook polenta
30g (1oz) butter
75g (2$\frac{1}{2}$oz) grated Parmesan cheese,
  plus extra to serve
freshly ground black pepper

METHOD

1 In a large saucepan, heat the stock until almost boiling.

2 Gradually whisk in the polenta, then continue to stir until the mixture is thick, but soft, adding a little more stock or water, if necessary.

3 Stir the butter and Parmesan into the mixture, and season to taste with black pepper. Scatter with a little more Parmesan, and serve immediately.

serves 4

prep 10 mins
• cook 10 mins

Grilled vegetables

Perfect for summer, these vegetables are easy to prepare and go well with any main dish.

INGREDIENTS

2 courgettes, halved lengthways
1 large red pepper, quartered
   lengthways and deseeded
1 large yellow pepper, quartered
   lengthways and deseeded
1 large aubergine, sliced
1 fennel bulb, quartered lengthways
120ml (4fl oz) olive oil,
   plus extra for brushing
3 tbsp balsamic vinegar
2 garlic cloves, chopped
4 tbsp coarsely chopped, flat-leaf parsley,
   plus extra to serve
salt and freshly ground black pepper

METHOD

1 Arrange the vegetables, cut-side up, in the non-metallic dish. Whisk together the oil, vinegar, garlic, and parsley, and season to taste with salt and pepper. Spoon over the vegetables and leave to marinate for at least 30 minutes.

2 Light the barbecue or preheat the grill on its highest setting. Grease the grill rack.

3 Lift the vegetables out of the marinade and place them on the barbecue or under the grill for 3–5 minutes on each side, or until tender and lightly charred, brushing with any extra marinade. Serve sprinkled with parsley, with any remaining marinade spooned over.

PREPARE AHEAD The vegetables can marinate for up to 4 hours. Or, cook the vegetables a day in advance and serve at room temperature.

serves 4

prep 20 mins,
plus marinating
• cook 4–6 mins

large, non-
metallic dish,
heat-resistant
pastry brush

Potato gratin

This regional French dish, *Gratin Dauphinoise*, is rich with cream and fragrant with garlic and nutmeg.

INGREDIENTS

45g (1¹/₂oz) butter, at room
   temperature, plus extra for greasing
900g (2lb) even-sized waxy potatoes
salt and freshly ground black pepper
600ml (1 pint) double cream
1 garlic clove, cut in half
pinch of freshly ground nutmeg

METHOD

1 Preheat the oven to 180°C (350°F/Gas 4). Butter the ovenproof gratin dish.

2 Peel the potatoes and slice them into even rounds, 3mm (¹/₈in) thick. Use the mandolin or food processor fitted with a fine slicing blade, if you have one. Rinse the potato slices in cold water, drain, and pat dry with kitchen paper or a tea towel.

3 Arrange the potatoes in layers in the prepared ovenproof dish. Season with salt and pepper.

4 Bring the cream to the boil in a saucepan with the garlic and nutmeg, then pour the cream over the potatoes. Dot the top with a few knobs of butter.

5 Cover and place in the oven for about 1–1¹/₂ hours, or until the potatoes are tender. During the last 10 minutes of cooking, remove the cover and increase the heat to get a fine golden crust on the top. Serve hot, straight from the oven.

PREPARE AHEAD The potatoes can be peeled and sliced several hours in advance and left in water.

serves 4–6

prep 15–20 mins
• cook 1½ hrs

mandolin or
food processor
fitted with fine
slicing blade,
21cm (8½in)
ovenproof
gratin dish

Ratatouille

This popular Mediterranean dish is delicious hot or cold.

INGREDIENTS

4 tbsp olive oil
1 onion, chopped
1 garlic clove, chopped
1 courgette, sliced
1 small aubergine, about 225g (8oz),
    cut into 2.5cm (1in) cubes
1 red pepper, cored, seeded
    and cut into 2.5cm (1in) pieces
150ml (5fl oz) vegetable stock
400g (14oz) can chopped tomatoes
2 tsp chopped oregano,
    plus 2–3 sprigs to serve
salt and freshly ground black pepper

METHOD

1 Heat the oil in a large casserole over moderate heat. Add the onion and cook for 5 minutes, until soft and transparent. Stir in the garlic, courgette, aubergine, and red pepper, and fry for 5 minutes, stirring.

2 Add the stock, tomatoes with their juice, and the chopped oregano to the casserole and bring the mixture to the boil. Reduce the heat to low and partially cover the pan. Cook until the vegetables are tender, stirring occasionally.

3 Season to taste with salt and pepper. Spoon the ratatouille into a serving bowl and serve immediately, garnished with oregano sprigs, or cover and refrigerate then serve cold.

serves 4

prep 15 mins
• cook 40 mins

Tabbouleh

This Lebanese speciality of parsley, mint, tomatoes, and bulgur is refreshing all year round.

INGREDIENTS

115g (4oz) bulgur wheat
juice of 2 lemons
75ml (2$\frac{1}{2}$fl oz) extra virgin olive oil
freshly ground black pepper
225g (8oz) flat-leaf parsley,
    coarse stalks removed
75g (2$\frac{1}{2}$oz) mint leaves, coarse
    stalks removed
4 spring onions, finely chopped
2 large tomatoes, deseeded and diced
1 head of Little Gem lettuce

METHOD

1 Put the bulgur wheat in a large bowl, pour over cold water to cover, and leave to stand for 15 minutes, or until the wheat has absorbed all the water and the grains have swollen.

2 Add the lemon juice and olive oil to the wheat, season to taste with black pepper, and stir to mix.

3 Just before serving, finely chop the parsley and mint. Mix the parsley, mint, and spring onions into the wheat.

4 Arrange the lettuce leaves on a serving plate and spoon the salad into the leaves.

serves 4

prep 20 mins,
plus standing

Spanish lentils

This classic Spanish dish of brown lentils, *Cocida de Lentejas*, relies on salty bacon, spicy chorizo, and paprika for its flavour.

INGREDIENTS

500g (1lb 2oz) brown lentils,
    washed and drained
2 bay leaves
85g (3oz) chorizo, cut into slices
    3cm (1¼in) in diameter
2 tbsp olive oil
2 garlic cloves, sliced
1 small slice of bread

salt
1 onion, finely chopped
75g (2½oz) thickly sliced tocino
    or streaky bacon, cut into strips
1 tbsp flour
1 tsp pimenton dulce (sweet paprika)
100ml (3½fl oz) vegetable stock

METHOD

1 Place the lentils in a large saucepan with 1 litre (1¾ pints) water, the bay leaves, and chorizo. Bring to the boil, then simmer for 35–40 minutes, or until the lentils are tender.

2 Meanwhile, heat 1 tbsp oil in a frying pan over a medium-low heat and fry the garlic, stirring, for 30 seconds, or until softened but not browned. Remove from the pan.

3 Add the bread to the pan and fry over a medium heat until lightly browned on both sides. Remove, place in a food processor along with the garlic, and season to taste with salt. Process to produce coarse crumbs.

4 When the lentils are cooked, drain, then return to the pan. Add the crumb mixture to the pan and stir until combined.

5 Add the remaining oil to the frying pan along with the onion and tocino. Fry for 3–4 minutes, or until the onion is soft and the bacon is cooked. Stir in the flour and pimenton dulce and cook, stirring, for 1 minute, then stir in the stock. Bring to the boil and simmer for 2 minutes, then stir into the lentils.

6 If necessary, add a little more stock or water, to moisten the lentils and heat through. Transfer to a heated serving dish.

PREPARE AHEAD The whole dish can be made 1 day in advance. Cover, chill, and reheat before serving.

serves 4

prep 15 mins
• cook 1 hr

Egg fried rice

This popular Chinese-style rice dish is an excellent way to use up leftover rice.

INGREDIENTS
1 tbsp groundnut oil or sunflower oil
1 onion, diced
1 green pepper or red pepper,
  deseeded and diced
500–675g (1lb 2oz–1½lb)
  cold cooked rice
2 eggs, whisked
2 tbsp soy sauce

METHOD
1 Heat the wok or a large frying pan over a high heat until very hot. Add the oil and swirl around. Add the onion and pepper and stir-fry for 3–5 minutes, or until softened but not coloured.

2 Add the rice to the pan and stir around until it is mixed with the vegetables and heated through. Push the rice away from the centre of the pan, pour in the eggs, and stir until scrambled and set.

3 Once the eggs are scrambled, toss all the ingredients together, add the soy sauce, and serve at once.

serves 4–6

prep 5 mins
• cook 10 mins

cook the rice
and chill rapidly,
or freeze until
ready to use

wok

Glazed carrots with thyme

These carrots are a perfect accompaniment to roast chicken.

INGREDIENTS
450g (1lb) carrots,
　　cut across into thin slices
thinly pared zest and juice
　　of 1 orange
25g (scant 1oz) butter
1 tbsp soft brown sugar
1 garlic clove, crushed
salt and freshly ground black pepper
½ tsp thyme leaves

METHOD
1 Place the carrots in a small saucepan with the orange zest and juice, butter, sugar, and garlic, and season to taste with salt and pepper. Add enough cold water to just cover the carrots.

2 Bring to the boil, then cover and cook over a moderate to high heat for about 8–10 minutes, or until the carrots are just tender.

3 Remove the lid and allow to bubble until all the liquid has evaporated and the carrots are glazed and golden at the edges, shaking the pan occasionally to prevent sticking. Just before serving, sprinkle over the thyme leaves.

PREPARE AHEAD Complete to the end of step 2 several hours in advance, then finish cooking just before serving.

serves 4

prep 10 mins
• cook 15 mins

Braised red cabbage with apple

Most cabbage varieties are best cooked quickly but red cabbage is an exception, benefiting from long, slow cooking.

INGREDIENTS

2 streaky bacon rashers, diced
1 onion, finely chopped
1 tbsp sugar
1 large tart apple, peeled,
    cored, and chopped
900g (2lb) red cabbage, quartered,
    cored, and shredded crossways
60ml (2fl oz) red wine vinegar
salt

METHOD

1 In a large frying pan or flameproof casserole, over low heat, fry the bacon until it renders its fat. Add the onion and cook for about 5 minutes, or until softened. Add the sugar and cook for 5 minutes, until the mixture is golden, then add the apple. Cover and cook, stirring from time to time, for 3–4 minutes.

2 Add the cabbage to the pan. Toss to coat thoroughly with the bacon fat, then stir in the vinegar and toss together. Cover the pan and cook over a low heat for 10 minutes, or until the cabbage changes colour.

3 Add salt to taste and 150ml (5fl oz) water. Cover and simmer over a medium-low heat, stirring occasionally, for 1–1¼ hours, or until the cabbage is very tender. Add a little more water, if necessary, to prevent the cabbage from drying out. Just before serving, season to taste with salt. Serve hot.

serves 4

prep 10 mins
• cook 1hr 25
mins–1 hr 40
mins

Ultimate mashed potatoes

Mash with a twist. This richly flavoured side makes a valuable contribution to the perfect roast dinner.

INGREDIENTS

1.35kg (3lbs) floury potatoes, such as
   King Edward or Maris Piper, peeled
2 tbsp double cream
2 tbsp milk
85g (3oz) butter
125g (4^1/$_2$oz) Cheddar cheese, grated
1 tbsp horseradish
4 spring onions, chopped
2 tbsp chopped parsley
2 tbsp chopped chives
salt and freshly ground black pepper

METHOD

1 Cut the potatoes into even-sized pieces. Place in a large pan and cover with water. Bring to the boil, add a little salt, then cover and simmer for 25 minutes, or until the potatoes can be pierced easily with a skewer or knife.

2 Remove from the heat and drain well.

3 Place the hot potatoes back into the pan with the cream, milk, and butter. Mash with a potato masher. Add the remaining ingredients, mix well, and serve.

serves 6

**prep 10 mins
• cook 45 mins**

ACKNOWLEDGMENTS

DORLING KINDERSLEY WOULD LIKE TO THANK THE FOLLOWING:

Photographers
Carole Tuff, Tony Cambio, William Shaw, Stuart West, David Munns, David Murray, Adrian Heapy, Nigel Gibson, Kieran Watson, Roddy Paine, Gavin Sawyer, Ian O'Leary, Steve Baxter, Martin Brigdale, Francesco Guillamet, Jeff Kauck, William Reavell

Picture Research
Emma Shepherd

Index
Susan Bosanko

224

Useful information

Roasting poultry

Use these times as a guide, bearing in mind the size and weight of each bird vary. Be sure to preheat the oven before cooking your bird(s), and always check that the bird is fully cooked before serving.

MEAT		OVEN TEMPERATURE	COOKING TIME
Poussin		190°C (375°F/Gas 5)	12 mins per 450g (1lb) plus 12 mins
Chicken		200°C (400°F/Gas 6)	20 mins per 450g (1lb) plus 20 mins
Duck		180°C (350°F/Gas 4)	20 mins per 450g (1lb) plus 20 mins
Goose		180°C (350°F/Gas 4)	20 mins per 450g (1lb) plus 20 mins
Pheasant		200°C (400°F/Gas 6)	50 mins total cooking
Turkey	3.5–4.5kg (7–9lb)	190°C (375°F/Gas 5)	$2\frac{1}{2}$–3 hrs total cooking
	5–6kg (10–12lb)	190°C (375°F/Gas 5)	$3\frac{1}{2}$–4 hrs total cooking
	6.5–8.5kg (13–17lb)	190°C (375°F/Gas 5)	$4\frac{1}{2}$–5 hrs total cooking

Oven temperature equivalents

CELSIUS	FAHRENHEIT	GAS	DESCRIPTION
110°C	225°F	$\frac{1}{4}$	Cool
130°C	250°F	$\frac{1}{2}$	Cool
140°C	275°F	1	Very low
150°C	300°F	2	Very low
160°C	325°F	3	Low
180°C	350°F	4	Moderate
190°C	375°F	5	Moderately hot
200°C	400°F	6	Hot
220°C	425°F	7	Hot
230°C	450°F	8	Very hot
240°C	475°C	9	Very hot